T0018321

RESTORE, RENEW, REBUILD

The life of Nehemiah and
the mission of Jesus

Cris Rogers
with Debra Green and Paul Weston

First published in Great Britain in 2022

Society for Promoting Christian Knowledge
36 Causton Street
London SW1P 4ST
www.spck.org.uk

British Library Cataloguing-in-Publication Data
A catalogue record for this book is available from the British Library

ISBN 978-0-281-08700-6
eBook ISBN 978-0-281-08701-3

1 3 5 7 9 10 8 6 4 2

Typeset by Falcon Oast Graphic Art Ltd
First printed in Great Britain by Ashford Colour Press

eBook by Falcon Oast Graphic Art Ltd

Produced on paper from sustainable sources

RESTORE, RENEW, REBUILD

The Revd Cris Rogers is Rector of All Hallows, Bow, London. Cris is a popular speaker and teacher at Spring Harvest, and has written ten books, including *The Bible Book by Book* (Monarch, 2012) and *Apprentice to Jesus* (SPCK, 2021).

Contents

Jesus is not in the business
of leaving people, things,
animals or atoms broken
and destroyed.
Jesus never shrugs and says,
'I guess I'm not really sure
what to do with this one!'
Jesus brings life from death,
beauty from ashes,
hope from despair,
light from darkness,
healing and hope from the
most broken, messed-up
and messy situations.
Jesus practises resurrection
with the rubble.

Foreword

Back in the fifth century BC, the people of God gathered together and began to rebuild the walls around Jerusalem that had been lying in ruins. Nehemiah is a beautiful and exciting story of God rebuilding ruins, and in turn, restoring the confidence of the people of God and renewing their faith in him.

This timely book will help us to address the challenges we face as we emerge from the crippling pandemic, to revitalise our Christian faith and the life of our churches. Cris Rogers has written this book with a deep passion for Scripture and a deep passion for the Church and the mission of Jesus. I have seen first-hand how Cris has been living the very content of this book over the last 12 years. In 2010, he and his family arrived at a church on the brink of closure. With a remnant congregation praying for their church, they have since seen new life, new growth, and two churches planted from their own church plant. The work of God is to see the ruins become something beautiful, and that vision is what you will find within these pages.

As you read this book, you will be confronted with challenging questions, and you will find the help to cast new vision with the inspiration to build a missional church for the future. All across the country, we are seeing God building up his Church, restoring and renewing in wonderful ways, and our prayer is that you and your community would be a part of this movement of hope and faith and love.

Ric Thorpe
Bishop of Islington and Director of the Gregory Centre (ccx.org.uk)

Introduction: a city of rubble

The last few years have left us feeling emotionally and physically surrounded by rubble. Many of us have lost loved ones to COVID-19 or had to navigate medical problems following recovery from infection with the virus. So many have lost jobs, and community life and friendships have been long-distance or had to be put on hold. Many of us have dipped or even sunk into mental health problems. Doubt has been knocking at the door. We feel fragile, broken and are longing for hope. Our hearts are aching for the world to go back to life as it was, while at the same time we know that it will never go back to 'normal'.

We find ourselves living in a new land; a land that we don't fully understand yet. However, it is into this landscape that the resurrection is promised, glimpsed and hoped for. The teachings of Rabbi Jesus and the writings found in the book of Revelation all point us to a hope for a future where heaven and earth come together in a new, radical and amazing way. Jesus teaches us that the kingdom is here, there and within. It is breaking in through the pavements of the very streets we walk on. God is doing a new thing. This is the hope and joy of the gospel.

Woven within the words of Scripture is God's promise of a new thing that he was doing. That new thing was Christ's resurrection but there was also the promise that his resurrection would be at work thereafter in people, things, animals and atoms. Isaiah put it powerfully in these words:

> See, I am doing a new thing!
>   Now it springs up; do you not perceive it?
> I am making a way in the wilderness
>   and streams in the wasteland.
> (Isaiah 43.19)

This new thing has been happening, is happening and will continue to happen right until the day Christ returns.

We have been here before. Humanity has been through the mill, pressed down and crushed many, many times throughout history. We see this powerfully in the story of Nehemiah. God's people had been removed from their homes, walls destroyed, protective gateways shattered and the glorious city of Jerusalem was merely a remnant of what it once was, surrounded by rubble. As we explore God's work in the world and the Church in this book, we will be doing so using the story of Nehemiah, looking at it through the lens of Jesus, his mission and the resurrection.

Nehemiah

The book of Nehemiah is a wonderful book that can (but shouldn't) be read as a standalone story. It's an historical event that sits within a wider story. Twelve years after the point at which the book of Ezra ends, Nehemiah hears that the holy city is still rubble. Originally, the Jews regarded the books of Ezra and Nehemiah as a single book. The opening of Ezra is also almost identical to the end of 2 Chronicles, which suggests that the authors are the same and this text is a supplement to the previous writing.

Nehemiah was a Jew living in exile, working for the king as a cup bearer, which was a highly respected position. It is not dissimilar to the work of a sommelier today. His role as cup bearer meant that Nehemiah would often have overheard information at the king's table that he would not have wanted his enemies to know. As a result, Nehemiah would have been seen as extremely trustworthy. His job was to protect the king from poisoning by drinking from the king's cup first. As a result, he became a confidant of the king and the trust between them meant that he also had great influence with King Artaxerxes.

The story of Nehemiah sits within a larger restoration story culminating in Jesus' death on the cross and his resurrection. We read the story of Nehemiah in the light of the story of Jesus and recognize that the rebuilding of Jerusalem is echoed by what Christ comes to do with the cosmos. The book of Nehemiah is a snapshot of what resurrection looks like to bricks and mortar, people and a city. Scripture then shows us what this looks like for the whole of humanity. As we read Nehemiah, we do so with Jesus at the front of our minds and, at the back of our minds, we ask the question, 'What does this look like now in the light of Jesus' resurrection?' What changes for us because of what Jesus has done? We must also remember that Nehemiah did not have Jesus or the work of the cross yet as a blueprint for his work. He didn't have the advantage of knowing what we now do.

Nehemiah restores the walls.

Jesus restores people, things, animals and the atoms. Churches, families, playgrounds, workplaces, medical centres and political structures.

1

GPS – locating the story of Nehemiah

We are now going to set the scene, giving a brief overview of the location and time in which the book of Nehemiah was written. It will also help us to understand the wider setting of the story. Don't worry, we will continue to dig deeper throughout the book, but here we will aim to grasp some of the initial issues.

Location one: Susa

The book of Nehemiah opens with a scene from the Persian capital city, Susa. It was typical of cities in the Persian Empire at that time – big and beautiful, with amazing architecture and grand statues lining the streets.

Susa, one of the oldest known settlements in Mesopotamia, was probably founded around 4000 BC as a small cluster of houses built on the top of a strategic hill. The little we know of its history suggests that it had a highly civilized culture. Susa grew from a fortified location, built with clay bricks, into a major city, linked by road with other capital cities, such as Ephesus, Sardis in Asia Minor and the sacred city of Persepolis, Persia's other great metropolis. The Persian Empire acquired many treasures from war and it is said that when Alexander the Great claimed the city in 323 BC, he needed in excess of 20,000 mules and 10,000 camels to take the treasures away.

Location two: Jerusalem

King Nebuchadnezzar, the Babylonian military leader, destroyed Jerusalem and Solomon's Temple in 586 BC, leaving the city decimated and in ruins. Many people still remained in the city once the Babylonians had left, but they made little effort to rebuild it. The city had been a powerful symbol of belief and identity and with this gone, the people were alone. This was a community lost in its own grief, unsure how to move forwards.

Nehemiah 1.3 paints a picture of the city as one with no walls or city gates and calls it a disgrace – not because of its appearance, but because it is a city that has no protection, so it could be conquered by anyone. The writer begins by comparing the impressive, educated culture of Susa to the derelict city of Jerusalem. It is this that helps us to contrast the two locations of the story: Persia, powerful, wealthy, strong, and Jerusalem, decimated and crushed. In Nehemiah 7, however, there is a shift: the walls have been finished and the gates put in place. The city has dignity again, but it is still considered incomplete because the ark of the covenant has gone missing.

Historical catch-up

During the period of exile, the people of Israel came to terms with their strange new home and developed a sense of what it meant to worship YHVH[1] away from Jerusalem and remain committed to their traditions. The faith that developed was no longer based on a location but on YHVH himself, so there was a shift in how he was worshipped and a growing understanding of him as the God of all creation. Their passion to worship YHVH helped them to form a new kind of Judaism, one based on the old but relating in a more

---

1 The name 'YHVH' is the name for the God of the Old Testament, as transliterated from the Hebrew consonants. You may well see it translated as 'JHVH', 'Yahve', 'Yahveh', 'Yahwe' or 'Yahweh'. In our English Bibles, it is simply rendered as 'LORD' or 'Lord'.

substantial way to the wider world. This new Judaism then came back to Jerusalem with Ezra, Nehemiah and the others returning home.

Three deportations

To understand the book of Nehemiah, we need to understand that there were three deportations of God's people. In 606 BC, the Babylonians deported the royal courts and the cream of society. At the time, they thought that this would subdue God's people in Jerusalem, but it didn't. This first deportation into exile included the teenage Daniel. The second deportation was of the craftspeople in 597 BC, which included Ezekiel. The final deportation, in 586, was of the rest of the Jewish people, when Babylonian warriors razed the Temple in Jerusalem to the ground. The city was left in ruins and the remaining tribes were exiled, all under the rule of the Babylonian king Nebuchadnezzar.

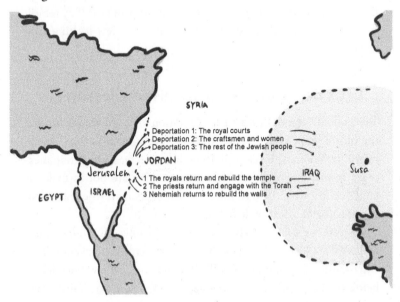

3

These three deportations were followed by three returns of God's people. First, Zerubbabel, in 537 BC. This brought back the royal line of David, and we find Zerubbabel mentioned in Matthew 1 as part of Jesus' family line. Zerubbabel's main concern was to revive the social and community life of Jerusalem, so the prince led the first people back, with the tribes of Judah and Benjamin.

Then Ezra followed in 458 BC. He returned the priests and a few Levites. Ezra's main concern was to revive the religious life of the city.

The final return came with Nehemiah, who was heartbroken to hear that the city was still in ruins, even though Ezra and the priests had returned. Remember, Nehemiah was a cup bearer; he was a lay person of high standing, not an architect nor a skilled builder. The rebuilding of the city of Jerusalem started to pick up steam not with the return of the religious leaders but by the prayerful man of God putting words into action. One of the powerful details of the book of Nehemiah is that it was a simple, prayerful man of God who moved into action. He went on to be the leader of the people as they rebuilt the city even though he started out as a simple Jew seeking God in prayer.

Let's be careful – a little history lesson . . .

The book of Nehemiah is a great inspiration for us as we look to what the future shape of the people of God, now known as the Church, might be. We must be careful, though, not to read the wrong messages from Nehemiah into our situation. We are not in exile, as God's people were then. Neither are we a theocracy, where a system of government priests rule in the name of God.

Instead, we find ourselves in what, arguably, is a *philosophical* exile. We are in a secular state that is growing increasingly hostile to Christianity. During the COVID-19 pandemic, we saw the Church being treated in similar fashion to a gym, cinema or hairdresser.

A secular society didn't understand or appreciate what the Church had to offer society in prayer and service and sidelined it as if it were an optional hobby activity.

We also need to remember that the book of Nehemiah, in its original form, was combined with the book of Ezra as a single book. If we put these two books together today, we end up reading Nehemiah differently. The story set out in Ezra *and* Nehemiah is that of three men who return to Jerusalem to restore it: Zerubbabel (Ezra 1 – 6), Ezra (Ezra 7 – 10) and Nehemiah (Nehemiah 1 – 7). Each one, however, makes mistakes, which creates conflicts in the process of the restoration, leaving each section of the story with a strange anticlimax. Essentially, although the people of God were returning to the city, they were still behaving with the same old heart that had led them into exile. It is this that makes the story so interesting for us.

What we will unpack in Nehemiah isn't the story of a perfect restoration project but the failure to correct the people's heart towards God's vision. As we read the whole book, we see this strange tale of very positive, religious and holy-looking decisions that, in fact, are questionable. Was rebuilding the wall what God wanted? Was he asking Nehemiah to do this or was it Nehemiah's decision? It could be argued that some of the choices he made may even have gone against what the prophets said. For example, King Zerubbabel acted strangely in the story by refusing unity and help. The Israelites who never went into exile came to help build the temple but Zerubbabel refused their help and told them that they were to have no part in the rebuilding. This was very odd as the prophets had spoken about all the tribes coming together alongside the people of all the nations. That is, the prophets spoke of unity but Zerubbabel refused this opportunity for unity. Later, it was all sorted out, but it was all rather weird.

Ezra learnt that many of the exiles had married non-Israelites. When they came back, they simply married non-Jewish women. Ezra turned to the Torah and, reading from Deuteronomy 23.1–4, came to the conclusion that the exiles who had done this were corrupt and would corrupt the people of God. To put this right, he led them in a heartfelt confession and commanded that these marriages should be dissolved and the women and children sent away, but only a few actually did this. However, God never commanded this and, in Malachi 2.13–16, the prophet said God was opposed to divorce. Ezra's actions led to chaotic results and a second anticlimax.

Nehemiah, like the other people in the story, wasn't quite like the character he is portrayed as being.

The prophet Zechariah said that the new Jerusalem would be a city without walls (see Zechariah 2.4, written in the sixth century BC, about 150 years before Nehemiah) and that people from all nations would come to worship and join the covenant people. However, Nehemiah operated according to a vision that was the entire opposite of this. Nehemiah was intent on building the walls back up and the workforce did not consist of people from all nations. In this section of the story, Nehemiah told the people surrounding Jerusalem that they had no part in the rebuilding of the walls. Nehemiah continued to build the city with integrity and courage but it certainly left a question as to whether this was God's vision or Nehemiah's.

Once all this had played out, Nehemiah and Ezra led the people of God in confession and brought about a spiritual renewal. In Nehemiah 8 – 12, we see them gathering everyone together for a festival where they read and taught the Torah, celebrated the feast of booths, confessed their sins, made a covenant with God and dedicated themselves to God's work.

However, Nehemiah 13 states that the people did not live out their covenant vows. They neglected the Temple and Zerubbabel's work was compromised (Nehemiah 13.4–13).

Ezra and Nehemiah's work was also compromised. The people set up market stalls and sold goods on the Sabbath. Again, the people swapped worship of God for worship of productivity and money.

Nehemiah responded in 13.25:

> I rebuked them and called curses down on them. I beat some of the men and pulled out their hair. I made them take an oath in God's name and said: 'You are not to give your daughters in marriage to their sons, nor are you to take their daughters in marriage for your sons or for yourselves.'

Did you see that? Nehemiah got violent!

People often connect this with Jesus clearing the money changers out of the temple in the Gospels, but what happened here is different. We see the desire for the buildings to be strong, for structures to be in place, but the lack of a desire to live out the life God is calling his people to.

In other words, God is looking for more from his people than building projects and surface-level structural differences. We can think that the renewal of the Church and its mission is about changing the style of worship, adding in a few more lights or a projector screen, but *this* story shows us that the people of God didn't need to rebuild the bricks and mortar; they needed to rebuild their hearts. They, like us, needed true, deep-down confession and repentance and a true commitment to God's ways.

Also demonstrated in Nehemiah is the illusion of perfect restoration – of both a better Jerusalem and a restored temple. It is easy to read the text through rose-coloured glasses but, like the city of Jerusalem, the Church has no perfect era. We can look at the early Church in Acts 2.42–47 as the perfect ideal of a church community, but we must remember that, even then, the Church was coloured by poor human decision-making and members lying. As we find inspiration in Nehemiah, we shouldn't do so to build the Church back up to what it *was*, but to build what is needed for the future mission and ministry of the Church. So much of Nehemiah is focused on bricks and mortar, but we must not miss that it is also focused on the reading of the Law and the realigning of the hearts of God's people, through confession to God (Nehemiah 8 and 9).

Therefore, we do not read Nehemiah with a mind to the 'restoration' of a golden era that never actually existed. We do so, looking at the patterns and vision laid out before us as we form a new shape for the Church in the UK. We are on the edge of a new, radical and adventurous apostolicity of the Church that is emerging.

We recognize that the kingdom of God is always future-shaped. The kingdom never looks backwards for its vision. Its trajectory is always towards the new heaven and the new earth. This means that, as we walk through the story of Nehemiah and what the people did in the book, we also have to remember that it's actually the book of Revelation that gives us a vision for the future. The people of Nehemiah didn't have this; they could only look back at old plans. We get to look forwards, to the new ones.

Why not . . .

In this book we are going to be talking about ourselves, the Church now and the Church of the future. In the process of doing this, we will be exploring the first three chapters of the book of Nehemiah as a framework to help us to build the Church going forwards. We recommend, however, that you read both the book of Ezra and the book of Nehemiah. That is because only the first half of Nehemiah's story is to be found in the book of Nehemiah and the second half is just as powerful, especially as it explores the rebuilding of culture and society. This whole rebuilding centres on the people of God re-committing to the word of God found in the Old Testament. As we journey together in this book, you will see recurring themes in your reading of both the book of Ezra and the book of Nehemiah.

Why not join us now, and read your Bible alongside?

Part 1

RESTORE

The words of Nehemiah son of Hakaliah:

In the month of Kislev in the twentieth year, while I was in the citadel of Susa, Hanani, one of my brothers, came from Judah with some other men, and I questioned them about the Jewish remnant that had survived the exile, and also about Jerusalem.

They said to me, 'Those who survived the exile and are back in the province are in great trouble and disgrace. The wall of Jerusalem is broken down, and its gates have been burned with fire.'
(Nehemiah 1.1–3)

2

Reality check: systemic sin

In the reality check chapters in each part of this book, the aim is to hear the prophetic voice loud and clear, so that we can explore where we, as the Church, need to make a change. Not everything here is for all of us, but it is worthwhile asking, 'What can we each do, as we play our part in the whole?'

Like Nehemiah, we need to apply a reality check to our current situation. As we will see in the story of Nehemiah, he has a reality check moment that brings great clarity. We, too, need such a moment.

The Church has been through a real season of change during the pandemic. We have moved from being mainly offline to online. We have learnt how to do church in person and on a TV screen. We have shifted from meetings in person to learning how to have them on Zoom, YouTube, Teams and other such platforms. We have discovered hybrid church: church both in person and online. Being church has moved from the pew to the sofa.

Let's be honest, before COVID-19, the majority of churches were doing the same thing on a Sunday (or midweek) that had been done for generations. The biggest shift for many of our churches up until then had been moving worship led by the organ to being led by the guitar – and we thought that was revolutionary! Since 2020, though, the Church has been changing and learning at rapid speed.

For many of us, as we start to think about the Church being restored, we rush to the golden moment in its past that we think was the perfect season. We must realize, however, that there are far more serious concerns that we need to deal with than worship style or presentation. The Church changing and growing isn't about being online or offline; it's about the very state and substance of the heart of the Church. Our biggest issue facing us . . . is us.

There is a lot in the Church's history that we need to recognize was shady, embarrassing and outright ungodly. The Church needs to have a rethink, reshape itself and ensure that it is restored to being in the likeness of Jesus. For many of us, our biggest worry is what our church worship style is like – 'Does it make me feel good? Do I get to serve in the way that I want to serve?' In reality, we have a heart issue, not a worship style issue.

We need to take a long hard look at ourselves and ask the question, 'Who have we been going to church for?'

God?

Those outside the Church?

Ourselves?

Let's be honest, for many of us – myself included – church can be, and has been, more about what *we* like than what *God* wants. We have been more concerned about the choice of songs than who is missing every week because they simply don't know or haven't heard the good news. We have been heartbroken when a service structure has been changed, something has been taken away or done differently, but quite unbothered by the poverty and injustice surrounding us.

As the Church – and that means me and you – we have massive, challenging issues in front of us. Before we face those issues, we must first confess our misguided certainty on agenda items without first listening to the Spirit. This isn't stating that we are wrong, but that our arrogant hearts have stopped us from listening, engaging with and responding to those we need to be listening to. Listening may mean changing our views but listening may also mean remaining in the same place but with a different heart.

We, as the body of Christ, need to ask ourselves, 'Have we been prideful in our hearts, positioning ourselves in self-preservation mode?' It could be that we have argued *our* corner without ever really asking what the other corners need, understand or stand on theologically. Could we be better listeners, truly hearing what someone else is saying rather than what we think that they are saying?

Every church has its own issues. Just like our individual struggles and strongholds, our church communities struggle or have their own areas of concern. In your church, there might be disagreements about a building project or a spirit of envy, pride or complacency. Perhaps you live in a community where there is a lot of debt or suicide rates are high and these are having an effect on your church. These should be identified, addressed and confessed individually as well as corporately. What I want to focus on here, though, are the larger issues that the Church with a big 'C' is struggling with and not addressing. What are we as the Church facing and not addressing? What are our major challenges and how are we coping?

Asking such questions may bring any given topic to mind. The big three, to my mind, are the environment, systemic racism and sexuality – namely, LGBTQ+. As soon as sexuality is mentioned in the Church, every single person looks to see if the person who brought it up agrees with their position or not. We seek to be validated by others or wonder if they are going to have 'that' view.

Please understand me, this is not a conversation about the theology of sexuality. We are not putting forward a view or asking for anyone else's. However, I would wager that your pulse has quickened just at the mention of the topic. Our responsibility as the Church is not simply to hold a theological position but, more importantly, to repent for how we have used our position or interpretation to hurt, isolate and scare people. We claim to be people who love but, too often, we have spoken and acted in ways that are harmful which have been wrapped in a false love.

The phrase 'I am telling you this because I love you' has often been used to mask our own true feelings of dislike, disapproval and even anger. Just because you say you love someone doesn't mean that your motives and actions are loving. The Church needs to repent for the barriers that we have created to stop people experiencing and encountering the wide, wide arms of Jesus – the arms that genuinely welcome them home.

We firmly stand by the traditional understandings of marriage and sexuality, but we also wholeheartedly want everyone to know about the radical, magnificent, transforming and redemptive love of Jesus. Jesus is the narrow way until you stand in the narrow way. Then you realize how wide the love and grace of Jesus is.

As the Church, we must confess the pain placed on people by what we call love. Such 'love', in actual fact, is oppressive and harmful. We must confess the times we focused on triumph in arguments rather than listening to people's pain.

Consumeristic and individualistic

The Church has drifted into a consumeristic and individualistic version of its former self, so we are no longer a family but consumers of Christian content. We consume the gospel for ourselves and fail to share it with others. We talk about a personal faith but what we mean is a consumeristic faith: 'What I want', 'What I get out of this'. Rather than a community, family, people of God and faith where we are adopted into a messy family with others who aren't like us, we treat church as a place where you *get* your feelings. Have you ever heard people say things like, 'I didn't get much out of that,' or 'I didn't really feel it today'? We make church about us and our needs, as opposed to a place of worship for our awesome God. Where does this consumer theology or thought come from?

It actually comes from a good place. When we come to Jesus, we are broken people so we have little to give, other than open hands and open hearts, which means that we receive so much more from him than we can ever give back. The trouble with this is that, if we stay here, then we can end up preaching a consumer faith. We can teach, 'Come and receive more from Jesus,' which is true and right, but we are also called to follow Jesus, copy Jesus and live for Jesus. We are called to work out our salvation each day.

Faith and action go hand in hand.

We have to confess that consumerism, rather than the Holy Spirit, can drive our decision as to which local church to attend. We must confess that, at times, we have sought out the sensational and mistaken it for spirituality. We substitute emotional and spiritual highs for real worship. Inspirational tweets replace Bible study. We search for seeker-friendly services rather than true evangelism.

Diversity

In the past few years we, the Church, have started to recognize the pain and hurt caused by long-term systemic racism going back generations. There seem to be two very distinct camps regarding this at present: we either grieve that we are still in this place and know that things must change radically or we actively, stubbornly and intentionally refuse to acknowledge it. In the Church, there is absolutely, unequivocally no place whatsoever for racism. We are one body and we are one people in Christ.

In Revelation 7.9 it is written, 'After this I looked, and there before me was a great multitude that no one could count, from every nation, tribe, people and language, standing before the throne and before the Lamb. They were wearing white robes and were holding palm branches in their hands.' As the body of Christ, we must confess, recognize and strive beyond platitudes to personally and corporately shape the Church so it looks like this heavenly picture.

It is our job – yours, mine, the Church as a whole – to make sure we live in ways that reflect this *now*, not just dream of it as a possibility in a future which never comes. We must not accept, nor entertain, racism in the Church, in church leadership – both ordained and lay – or in our communities. We must play our part in being the diverse people of God, growing leaders of all ethnicities and ages. We must make a promise to call out any attitudes and behaviours that do not promote the fullness of God in humanity. To respond and recognize that there are times we have got it wrong requires confession as well. We must ask for forgiveness and do better. It is vital that we acknowledge our shame regarding institutional racism within each of our denominations. We must also make a covenant to continue to challenge and address issues of racism and inequality within the wider Church.

Alongside racial diversity, we have neglected other forms of diversity within the Church – in terms of age, gender, disability and others. We must do better. We are called to do better. Let us allow space for these to be named and respond in the same way that Jesus would. That, quite simply, is our role as the Church.

Abuse

We recognize that child and vulnerable adult abuse has been perpetrated in the Church, in every denomination. When anyone is harmed by someone in church leadership of any kind, it doesn't hurt just the denomination concerned but also the whole body of Christ, and Christ himself.

We must confess that the Church has turned a blind eye, we have allowed predators to continue and have failed to support those who have been victims. The reason this is still an issue today is because we, as the Church, have refused to deal with it honestly thus far. It has to end now.

We need to stop and confess

If we are to see the Church once more filled with the Holy Spirit, with Christ at its centre, its people loved, saved and commissioned to make disciples in all areas of our lives, then we must recognize that this begins with us getting down on our knees, confessing our sin, repenting of our shameful ways and receiving forgiveness from God and others. This is because, when you have had an argument with someone, you can't ignore what has happened and pretend like everything is OK. There is a palpable tension. You must deal with the argument, sort out the problem and seek forgiveness. It is the same for us personally with God but also with the Church, the body of Christ and God.

Note: If you have been affected by any of the topics discussed in this section, please speak with someone you trust who cares for you. Do not give up. You are deeply loved.

3

Nehemiah 1: disruption, heartache and confession

When I heard these things, I sat down and wept. For some days I mourned and fasted and prayed before the God of heaven. Then I said:

'LORD, the God of heaven, the great and awesome God, who keeps his covenant of love with those who love him and keep his commandments, let your ear be attentive and your eyes open to hear the prayer your servant is praying before you day and night for your servants, the people of Israel. I confess the sins we Israelites, including myself and my father's family, have committed against you. We have acted very wickedly towards you. We have not obeyed the commands, decrees and laws you gave your servant Moses.

'Remember the instruction you gave your servant Moses, saying, "If you are unfaithful, I will scatter you among the nations, but if you return to me and obey my commands, then even if your exiled people are at the farthest horizon, I will gather them from there and bring them to the place I have chosen as a dwelling for my Name."

'They are your servants and your people, whom you redeemed by your great strength and your mighty hand. Lord, let your ear be attentive to the prayer of this your servant and to the prayer of your servants who delight in revering your name. Give your servant success today by granting him favour in the presence of this man.'

(Nehemiah 1.4–11)

Disruption and restoration

The book of Nehemiah starts by setting the scene, which helps us to situate it within a location and timescale. It then, but very quickly, moves us on to Nehemiah's opening prayer. It's this prayer that helps us to understand two things. First, we learn that Nehemiah's heart was a prayerful one. When Nehemiah heard about the city of Jerusalem and the physical state of the walls and gates, he was moved to pray about the problem.

Second, we learn more about the place of prayer and confession in the wider story. Nehemiah didn't simply pray for the physical construction project but also recognized the sin that had led the city to a place of destruction. Prayer and confession therefore sit at the heart of this first chapter of Nehemiah.

There is also a structure and outline for prayer within Nehemiah's prayer. The Jewish people taught spiritual disciplines not simply through a step-by-step guide but also by telling stories of how those disciplines were to be used. We, as readers, are to take in Nehemiah's prayer, be inspired by it and use his outline for our own prayers.

The place of heartbreak

In chapter one of Nehemiah, we read that it was the month of Kislev in the twentieth year that he prayed to God. In chapter two, as we start to see the answer to his prayer, we are told that it is the month of Nisan, which was four months later. The full answer to Nehemiah's prayer and confession didn't come until some time later. We often want quick answers to our prayers, but God brings perfectly timed answers.

If we take a further look at the two months mentioned in Nehemiah, a spiritual picture is also being painted. Say I told you that I prayed in winter and the answer came in the spring. You could easily associate the seasons with what was happening to me spiritually, and that is what is happening in the passage too. Nehemiah was praying in the month of Kislev, located around November and December in today's diaries (early winter there). There would have been snow on the mountains and it would have been bitterly cold. The answer to Nehemiah's prayer started to come in the month of Nisan, which would have seen the first fruits of the barley crop and the falling of the spring rains.

Nehemiah prays in the winter.

Nehemiah sees some movement towards an answer in the spring.

This gives us a spiritual picture of what God was doing. Chapter 2 in Nehemiah shows the 'spring' of the problem, that change was coming.

The lesson the passage offers us is to start with prayer, but we must also have the patience to wait for the Lord's answer, which will come at whatever time he ordains. Sometimes in people's frustration with the Church they start with prayer but grow impatient and don't wait for the response. This behaviour partly stems from a desire to see change, but the danger of this starting point is that we will check out if we don't see movement. Indeed, some churches have been established as a result of frustration felt in other churches and denominations rather than a real calling and love. Nehemiah's prayer for Jerusalem, however, came from a heartfelt love for the city. His heart was broken when he heard about the state it was in. This heartbreak moved him to prayer and petition, which continued until the king noticed his pain and then he was able to see movement in his situation. Nehemiah could have prayed, eventually become frustrated and given up. He could simply have seen it as a situation that could not be changed, but he did not.

God's heartbreak

In the same way that we looked at how Nehemiah prayed, let's look at how our heavenly Father responded to the same situation. God was heartbroken too. Indeed, Nehemiah mirrored God's heartbreak. The whole period of the exile opens up the significant issue of God's presence in suffering, trauma and destruction. Was God happy to sit back and watch as horrific things happened to his people? The simple answer is no. God was grieving with his children as he saw them taken into exile. He grieved for the city, its people and their needs.

In Jeremiah 9.10, the writer spoke directly about this period of time and God expressed his grief, with a broken heart for his people:

> I will weep and wail for the mountains
>   and take up a lament concerning the wilderness grasslands.
> They are desolate and untravelled,
>   and the lowing of cattle is not heard.
> The birds have all fled
>   and the animals are gone.

Feeling this deep heartbreak, God called for his people to see (publicly) what was happening in his heart (hidden). At that time, as in many cultures before and after, men and women of great stature had professional mourners, who were employed to follow behind the coffin in the burial procession. These professionals made such a noise that there would be no question as to the person's importance or the pain the grievers felt. Further on in the chapter, God calls for his people to do this, to act out his grief publicly so that his heartache can be seen:

This is what the LORD Almighty says:

> 'Consider now! Call for the wailing women to come;
>   send for the most skilful of them.
> Let them come quickly
>   and wail over us
> till our eyes overflow with tears
>   and water streams from our eyelids.'
> (Jeremiah 9.17–18)

God wanted to make sure that his people knew he was not OK about their situation, that what they felt, he was feeling also.

A few years ago, I received a postcard, and written on the front were these words, which I found really helpful:

God is not in the business of leaving things broken and messy. He's not a God who sees a hard situation, shrugs and says, 'I guess I'm not really sure what to do with this one.' He's a God who brings life from death, beauty from ashes, hope from despair. Light from darkness and healing from the most broken, messed-up and messy situations.

How do we keep the passion and heartbreak for the Church in prayer?

When I heard these things, I sat down and wept. For some days I *mourned* and *fasted* and *prayed* before the God of heaven. (Nehemiah 1.4, italics added)

Nehemiah sat down and '*bakah*' for some days. This Hebrew word is translated here as 'wept', which is certainly better than simply 'cried', but it would be more accurate to say 'bewailed' or 'wailed'. Nehemiah was heartbroken about the situation and his response was to wail, lament and sob for days over it. *Bakah* is the act of deeply sobbing for a long period of time. Strong's concordance says it's a weeping that is continuous and felt deep down.

The reality of a true, deep-down heartbreak will always leave us aching. Surface-level heartbreak or obligatory heartbreak is short-lived. Real heartbreak takes us to a thin place where we can meet God in a wholly unique way. It also calls for endless, consuming time in prayer.

We only pray persistently for something that we continually desire over time.

Surface-level desire will wane with time as other things replace it, but deep heartbreak will lead us to a life lived in prayer for the issue in hand. Those who have lost a loved one will often say that grief changes over time, but the pain of the loss is always present. The love also remains.

It was such deep-down heartbreak that led Nehemiah to a healthy place of mourning, fasting and praying. This is a helpful response for us to learn from as we look at the Church. Learning to grieve well for the history of the Church, for where we have fallen short, fasting for the Church and then praying for the Church will start to shift us to a better place. Nehemiah's grief led him to repentance and then action. We, too, need such a moment to experience grief for the past and its failings and then also to move on to repentance and confession, which will then allow us to progress forwards to action.

'Hang on, though,' you might ask, 'are you really saying that we should grieve for the past history of the Church?' Our answer would be, 'Yes, we are.' There are so many things that we need to take into account, as they have affected and shaped the Church of the present and will shape the Church of the future. We have to grieve the ways in which Christians have behaved with regard to race, wealth, sexual abuse, misuse of power and so on. Unless we feel the pain of who we have become and how we got here, we will not have the right motivation to bring about change, growth and to rebuild the Church.

Mourn, fast and pray

Nehemiah's foundation for what came to pass was to mourn, fast and pray for the city. This foundation of spiritual disciplines became the biblical launching pad for the vision and God's ordained activity. The Bible offers many examples of how we should prepare for, and even petition, God for these movements, but here are two.

- **Matthew 4** Here, we see Jesus about to launch his ministry. Before he does, he steps into 40 days of prayer and fasting.

- **Acts 13.2–3** In this passage, we see the launching of the Church into the world. Through worship, prayer and fasting, the disciples were able to set a vision and choose Paul and Barnabas to lead the launch.

Throughout the Old Testament and ancient Judaism, too, we see this rhythm of mourning, repentance, prayer and fasting in the hope that God will respond with his presence and power. Fasting for the ancient Jewish community was a sign that something was wrong. Eating is a normal part of human life, so abstinence is a disruption to the very rhythm of life. Within this same tradition is also the idea that fasting and abstinence from food point us to something more necessary for life than food: communion with and dependence on God.

The Hebrew Bible consistently portrays fasting in conjunction with themes of disruption and restoration. With mentions of fasting and prayer there is a sense of hope, that things can change when God is involved, and there is a renewal of a relationship with him and his sustaining force.

The acts of prayer and fasting are described in the Scriptures as together, then supercharging what follows. Fasting, traditionally, was added to intercession as an effective means of strengthening the force of prayer. It takes the person fasting out of the centre of decision-making and makes them more receptive to what God is planning.

Nehemiah's holy discontent moment could have led him, like others, to respond and act right away. It can be the same for us when we have a vision in mind. Our first decisions and thoughts always seem like good ones, but they might not be. Taking the time to fast and pray allows us to focus on God rather than ourselves. Fasting and praying always slows us down, takes us out of the centre of things, leaving us room to pick up on divine direction and openings.

Fasting and praying in this way will always lead us, as it did Nehemiah, to a place of saying yes to being the answer to our own prayers. As Nehemiah found through fasting, he was the answer to his prayer and God gave him the route to do it. By fasting and praying, we allow ourselves to find out if we are indeed God's answer. By fasting and praying like Nehemiah, we say no to work and productivity for solely our own ends. We are tempted to keep working things out under our own steam, but fasting makes sure that we say no to doing this. Fasting helps us to say no to unethical practices that cause us to cut corners. It helps us to keep away from inappropriate emotional relationships that distract us from the task in hand. Fasting helps us to behave in a way that is correct for our character when it comes to dealing with whatever God has laid on our hearts and whatever it was that took us to the place of fasting at the outset.

If we want to work and act in a way that aligns with what God has planned and set a vision for, then to pray and fast will keep us in line with this rather than our own earthly, human opinions.

- Fasting helps us to adopt appropriate habits that will make us receptive to God's plans and movements. (Note how, in Nehemiah 2, he quickly saw the opening he had to talk to the king.)
- Fasting will expand our interior lives so, rather than being anxious, we will place our feet on a spacious place and find peace.
- Through fasting we will gain clarity of vision and strategy.
- Through fasting our hearts will align with what is in God's heart and our hearts will break for what breaks God's heart.

How to confess and intercede for the Church

To help us as we explore how we can confess and intercede on behalf of the Church, praying for its future, we return to Nehemiah. He gives us the structure for a prayer of this kind that is far more detailed than the Lord's Prayer. His great prayer helps us to see how we need to engage with God in prayer.

Let's walk through the structure of Nehemiah's prayer in chapter 1 (see Table 2.1).

Table 3.1 The structure of Nehemiah's prayer

Praise	'LORD, the God of heaven, the great and awesome God, who keeps his covenant of love with those who love him and keep his commandments.' (Nehemiah 1.5)	We begin our prayer by acknowledging that we stand before Almighty God. He is the powerful one, all things are held in his hands. We need to approach prayer with great respect and deep reverence. It's a mutual partnership, his covenant of love meeting our covenant to keep his commands, though we always end up failing to do so. Because of Jesus, however, we approach him boldly, with confidence, but prayerfully, not pridefully. By praying first with praise, we recognize our powerlessness and our complete dependence on him. It also fixes our agenda on him.	Who is God? What has he done? What is his character?
Position	'Let your ear be attentive and your eyes open to hear the prayer your servant is praying before you day and night for your servants, the people of Israel.' (Nehemiah 1.6a)	Nehemiah realized that one individual plus God is a majority in every situation. With this in mind, he approached God, asking for his direct attention, and set out his needs. Nehemiah positioned himself and Israel as servants of God. Taking this position was essential for understanding the will of God. We need to pray in tune with God, not against him. In prayer, Nehemiah identified himself as God's humble servant and asked for success as he went	Who are we before God? What is our position? What is our duty?

about God's business. Prayer is not an excuse for inaction. It does not absolve us of the responsibility to act. When we pray, we are reporting for duty. We must be ready to surrender, to make sacrifices and to serve.

Nehemiah knew that God was always paying attention to him but didn't want to take any chances, so he specifically asked God to listen out for him. This reveals to us his anxiety and commitment.

At the heart of Nehemiah's prayer are confession and penitence. Nehemiah openly admitted that both he and the people of God had sinned. He set out the lie of the land, confessing:

- their actions against God;
- that they had disobeyed his commands.

Remember, at this point, Nehemiah was a cup bearer for the king and he was taking responsibility for all his people. In confession we, too, can choose to pray for the whole Church, in its widest sense. Nehemiah also prayed for the people of God who didn't realize that they had broken any commands. He held in his prayer every attitude, desire and will.

What do we need to confess?

Who do we need to confess on behalf of?

What do we need to confess ourselves?

Penitence 'I confess the sins we Israelites, including myself and my father's family, have committed against you. We have acted very wickedly towards you. We have not obeyed the commands, decrees and laws you gave your servant Moses.'
(Nehemiah 1.6b–7)

Promises	'Remember the instruction you gave your servant Moses, saying, "If you are unfaithful, I will scatter you among the nations, but if you return to me and obey my commands, then even if your exiled people are at the farthest horizon, I will gather them from there and bring them to the place I have chosen as a dwelling for my Name."' (Nehemiah 1.8–9)	Reminding God of his promises is an excellent way to pray. As we do so, we remind ourselves of those promises. We engage with our own hope that we felt when we first heard God's promises. When we pray and speak out the promises anew, it helps us to reconnect with what they mean and why they are important to us. God is fully aware of his promises, but when we remind him, he knows that we are serious and it deepens our connection with him, strengthening the relationship.	What are the promises God has made to us? How do we respond to those promises? What happens to our levels of hope and faith as we remind ourselves of the promises?
Petition	'They are your servants and your people, whom you redeemed by your great strength and your mighty hand. Lord, let your ear be attentive to the prayer of this your servant and to the prayer of your servants who delight in revering your name. Give your servant success today by granting him favour in the presence of this man.' (Nehemiah 1.10–11)	Nehemiah repeated his prayer request, asking for God's attentive ear and then asking for success. Nehemiah asked God for help, but also saw himself as possibly being the answer to that prayer. In this, Nehemiah petitioned God for success and favour in the eyes of the king. He asked God to provide the way forward and ensure success for what he was about to do.	What needs to be underlined, not only for God's benefit but also for ours? For what areas of your life do you need to ask for success? Where do you need God's favour?

Let's take note

Though there is much information and inspiration to be found in Nehemiah's prayer, we now want to focus on a few points as we learn to fast and pray for the Church.

- In Nehemiah's prayer, lament led him to hope. As we lament, we also need to have hope for the Church. God has not finished with her yet. The Church is God's 'Plan A' and we must have hope for a new future, centred on the various communities within our nation.
- From Nehemiah we learn that repentance is key to the restoration process. Real repentance and responsibility for our actions is part of how we can restore our relationship with God. If we try to make changes without repentance, we are only playing with sticking plasters. Repentance takes us to a deeper place to enable reconnection with God.
- Nehemiah teaches us to take responsibility for our own failings in our prayer and fasting, not someone else's. He could have chosen a different leader in Jerusalem to fast, confess and pray on behalf of, but he didn't. Nehemiah took it on himself and recognized that he was part of the problem.
- In Nehemiah's prayer, we can see that God is looking for the transformation of our hearts. He is searching for a repentant heart, a reconnected heart.

Prayer and fasting, then, set the tone for the future. They set the vision and direction for our relationship with God and the future strategy.

One thing changes everything

We must not forget that we have something Nehemiah didn't: Christ Jesus. Throughout the story of Nehemiah, he tried to keep the people of Israel from sinning. Until the very end of the book, however, they kept slipping back into the habits of greed and worshipping the wrong things. Nehemiah strived to make a difference, but he was trying to do the work of the cross without the cross.

The story of the city with broken walls, filled with sinful people, is the story of the Church, but it is also the story of us. We each have broken walls, we try to drink from broken wells and we are full of sin. No matter how hard we try, we will always come back to being broken people.

> The city is full of sinners.
> The Church is full of sinners.
> I am in the Church,
> but the city and the Church also now have a Messiah, a Saviour . . . Christ Jesus.

This means that, for us to see the restoration of the Church, its worship, its place in society and people saved, we need to find forgiveness in Jesus Christ and the Church needs to be saved by grace through faith in Jesus.

As Paul expresses it in Ephesians 2.8, 'For it is by grace you have been saved, through faith – and this is not from yourselves, it is the gift of God.' The Church has been saved by Jesus for Jesus and his mission and vision.

Also, from the New Testament, in 1 John 1.9, 'If we confess our sins, he is faithful and just and will forgive us our sins and purify us from all unrighteousness.' We have Jesus, which means that we can express our sin with confidence, knowing that his grace will meet us right in the place of need.

Identificational repentance

We can very easily have problems confessing sins that we have not committed. This difficulty typically is more pronounced in the West than it is in the East. In the West, people tend to think much more of themselves as single individuals and be more focused on the self than is the case in other parts of the world. Culturally, there is therefore less of a focus on community and people generally take less care of those outside their immediate family or social group. The Western way of life is to be pretty self-reliant and is structured around the self; there is not a strong sense of communal responsibility, so if something doesn't affect people personally, they tend to think that it's not really a problem. Conversely, in the East, life is much more communal and so there is an understanding of the impact of communal and systemic sin and, in turn, the need for us to confess it.

One difficulty that comes up in relation to identification repentance is that of identifying with a faceless organization. For example, if you worked for a large corporation and received a letter stating that it was letting you go, you might struggle to be angry with the corporation as it would only be identified as a name or logo. However, you would be angry with the sender of the letter and the managers you worked for. In the same way, the Church and society are largely faceless – a massive family and community. As we are each representatives of that community, however, like the sender of the letter or the managers at the corporation, we must own the actions of the Church as a whole as we are a part of its body. As we enjoy the privileges of the body, we must also own its problems.

Nehemiah understood his part in the problems of the wider community of which he was a member. The principle of identificational repentance is that prayers of confession and prayers of intercession merge into a heart cry for God to pour out his Spirit on the Church. As we look back on the Church's history, we can see that, where there has been a groundswell of this type of prayer, there has followed a significant move by God.

The word 'identificational' in this context means a willingness to join ourselves to a group of people and to be counted as one of them. Identificational *repentance*, therefore, means a willingness to identify ourselves with the sins of a group of people. The sins of:

our family
our church
our denomination
our gender
our race
our tribe
our nation
our class and upbringing
our economic position
our humanity in relation to impact on climate.

We then repent of the sins of these and other groups, even though we may not be personally responsible for them. We do this by owning these sins as ours and repenting of them on behalf of those who are unready or unable to do this themselves. It can help to repent of sins with which you can identify or imagine yourself committing in similar circumstances.

If you need a biblical example of this, look no further than the cross. That is exactly what Jesus did for us all on the cross.

Nehemiah knew that all the greatest wounds, corruption and injustices committed by the people of God were not the acts of a single individual, but resulted from the family inflicting their sinful hearts on one another and those around them. Nehemiah also knew that people, in all their humanity, were tempted to clear their own consciences by distancing themselves from having any personal responsibility for those sins. The same is true today.

Nehemiah could have looked at the situation the people of God were in and found others to blame – 'It's his or her fault,' 'He or she did X,' 'He or she neglected to do Y.' Similarly, we as the Church today could look at our situation and place blame by pointing the finger at those who have deviated from, neglected, abandoned and corrupted the Church in the past.

Nehemiah chose to take the mistakes made by the people of God on as his responsibility and his mistakes. Nehemiah knew that if it wasn't him and his generation that had made 'those' particular choices, they would do. As individuals in the Church, we, similiarly, need to choose to take on the mistakes of the Church as our responsibility. If past generations hadn't made those bad decisions, then we certainly would do.

Nehemiah understood that if he didn't pray in this way on behalf of the people, how could he expect the healing and reconciliation to come. Let's make it clear, identificational repentance is not about our own personal culpability before God for sins that we have committed. Jesus has dealt with those as we have confessed them. Rather, this is about recognizing what has happened in the past of our churches and communities that has led us to the situation we are in now and asking God, in penitence and faith, to grant new mercy and favour that will mend and remake our context. If we, as believers, do not do this on behalf of our people, to confess the wrongs committed, how will healing and reconciliation come to us?

Nehemiah was not the only one to do this. Another example is Daniel. Notice how he confessed in the same way that Nehemiah did:

So I turned to the Lord God and pleaded with him in prayer and petition, in fasting, and in sackcloth and ashes.

I prayed to the LORD my God and confessed:

'Lord, the great and awesome God, who keeps his covenant of love with those who love him and keep his commandments, *we* have sinned and done wrong. *We* have been wicked and have rebelled; *we* have turned away from your commands and laws. *We* have not listened to your servants the prophets, who spoke in your name to our kings, our princes and our ancestors, and to all the people of the land.

'Lord, you are righteous, but this day we are covered with shame – the people of Judah and the inhabitants of Jerusalem and all Israel, both near and far, in all the countries where you have scattered us because of our unfaithfulness to you. *We* and our kings, our princes and our ancestors are covered with shame, LORD, because *we* have sinned against you. The Lord our God is merciful and forgiving, even though *we* have rebelled against him; *we* have not obeyed the LORD our God or kept the laws he gave us through his servants the prophets. All Israel has transgressed your law and turned away, refusing to obey you.

'Therefore the curses and sworn judgments written in the Law of Moses, the servant of God, have been poured out on us, because we have sinned against you.'

(Daniel 9.3–11, italics added)

Daniel identified with the people of God by using the world 'we' in his prayer and confession to God. Likewise, we need to ask, 'Am I willing to be a part of this reconciliation?'

Nehemiah knew that, until the heart had confessed and the sin had been dealt with, anything built would have been built on a foundation of sin and corruption of the heart. Once the confession had happened, however, and reconciliation with God had begun, then the building could happen based on a clean heart and a pure mind.

Only then would the foundations be good.

4

Yes, but how?

With Debra Green and Paul Weston

Having explored the theme of confession and repentance in the previous chapter, let us now take some time to get practical!

For our hearts to be restored, we must acknowledge our brokenness and the brokenness around us, just as Nehemiah did. Before we can rebuild, though, we must stand in the rubble and feel the pain. The tension for us is that we might know we need to confess and repent but struggle to work out how we are to go about it. It's much easier for us to spot what needs to be confessed by others than it is to spot it in ourselves.

As we have seen so far in Part 1, this is a process rather than a one-off event. It involves reflection, mourning, confession, repentance, fasting, prayer and lament. During this time, we align our hearts to the Father's and our will to his will. We become reliant on God, not on our own solutions, we humble ourselves before him and allow him to bring healing. Our confession includes repenting of not only our own sins but also those of previous generations. We take responsibility for what went wrong.

There are practical steps that we need to take to prepare our hearts.

Recognizing brokenness

By 'brokenness', we mean the broken state of our hearts, our need for surrender and the defeat we experience when hardship rocks our existence. Sometimes this is the result of sin, which can be our sin or someone else's. We each have to acknowledge to ourselves the fact that 'I, too, am a sinner who needs to be saved.' Our sin causes our lives to be dysfunctional and our relationship with God to be broken.

We must start by recognizing our sinful selves, that we need the Saviour, not just others, and we have caused our own lives and the lives of others to become dysfunctional and broken by sin.

As we have seen, Nehemiah's heart was broken by the plight of Jerusalem. He allowed God to break his heart. He then could identify with the sin of Jerusalem and take responsibility for it. To start to understand and feel God's heart, which is also broken in pain for other situations his people endure, we must allow the Spirit to reveal to us the heart of God.

How can I recognize the brokenness in my heart and situation?

- Ask God to reveal how you have sinned or hardened your heart towards him and others.
- Invite the Holy Spirit to be present with you and be open to what the Spirit reveals.
- Bring these things to the Father in prayer.
- Identify with the pain of others.
- Allow yourself to weep.

Identifying sin

Take some time to pause and ask yourself, as you invite the Holy Spirit, 'What is the sin and brokenness in my heart?' What can you identify that needs to be confessed?

Also take time to reflect on society. What is the sin within society that, ultimately, is going to cause its destruction? Once you have done this, ask yourself if there is anything at the heart of society that you, too, need to own. It might be that you are blinded to your own state, so you might like to ask the Lord to reveal this to you.

Yes, but how?

IDENTIFY THE SIN
IN YOUR OWN HEART

IDENTIFY THE SIN
IN SOCIETY'S HEART

Retreat from busyness

He said to them, 'Come with me by yourselves to a quiet place
and get some rest.'
(Mark 6.31)

Our lives are so busy and cluttered that it is often difficult to be
aware of what it is that the Lord wants to reveal to us. The psalmist
in Psalm 46.10 said, 'Be still, and know that I am God.' It's good to
take time out from everyday life and spend it alone in his presence.
This can be at home or some other place where you feel able to access
his presence.

Can you physically remove yourself from your everyday sur-
roundings? A retreat is a great way to get alone time with God.
Defined simply as time (from a few hours in length to a month)
spent away from one's normal life for the purpose of reconnecting,
usually in prayer, with God, a retreat can mean simply going into
your or someone else's garden or else going on an actual break or
other form of removal from typical daily life.

- Choose a time of day or a day in the week when you can simply
  be still.
- Listen. You can say, 'I am listening Lord, please speak,' or pray,
  but be still and quiet also.
- Write down anything that comes to you. It is good to keep a prayer
  journal to record your prayers and the answers you receive.

Rhythms of prayer

Everyone is unique and there are many ways to practise a rhythm
of prayer. Find one that feels right for you but don't feel discour-
aged if the first thing you try doesn't work for you. Be liberated from
the expectations of others and find your own prayer rhythm. This
might include prayer walking, memorizing Scripture, meditation

on God's word, silence, listening, quick-fire arrow prayers, liturgy, observing nature and God's creation.

There are many beautiful prayers that have been written over the centuries and it can be very rewarding to choose some to recite and use to centre your thoughts on a loving heavenly Father who longs to restore your heart. *Celtic Prayers from Iona* by J. Philip Newell (Paulist Press, 1997) is a good place to start.

Here are some other ideas for things you could try that you might find helpful.

- Set aside a regular time. It may feel uncomfortable at first, but as you repeat the practice regularly, it will soon become part of your life.
- Find materials that inspire you (see, for example, the Lectio 365 resource on 24-7 Prayer's website at: <https://24-7prayer.com/dailydevotional>)
- Ask yourself, do I relate best to the written word or spoken word? To music or art?
- Do you prefer to sit quietly or be active? Try combining prayer with an activity, such as gardening or walking.
- Be careful not to make comparisons between how you and others practise a rhythm of prayer. Be yourself and do things that work best for you.
- There are some excellent books around, and we recommend the following to you: Brian Heasley's *Be Still* (SPCK, 2021), *How to Pray*, by Pete Greig (Hodder & Stoughton, 2019), and *Mountain-Moving Prayer*, by Debra Green (SPCK, 2019).

Confession and repentance

The idea of personal confession is central to the Christian faith. It is part of the process of repentance and necessary in order for hearts to be restored and reconciled with Almighty God.

Confession involves admitting and acknowledging something that people would prefer to keep hidden, because they know that they have done something wrong, intentionally or accidentally. In the Judeo-Christian tradition, the acknowledgement of sin in public or private is regarded as necessary to obtain God's forgiveness: 'If we confess our sins, he is faithful and just and will forgive us our sins and purify us from all unrighteousness' (1 John 1.9).

There is a difference between confession (naming the sin) and repentance (walking away from sin). When we confess, we must then also walk away from our sinful behaviour and put in place practices that will keep us from doing it again in the future.

There are five important stages in the process of moving from confession to repentance. We can use these to help us establish a regular pattern, each step enabling us to walk further away from sins we've committed in the past.

- **Name the sin** You may want to write it down – you could do so in the heart shapes on page 39. Whether it is your sin or not, you know what has been done. By labelling it, you are a step closer to acknowledging it. You don't have to broadcast it, but you do have to know that it's there yourself. Putting a name to it makes it real – simply saying, 'I have done wrong,' is not enough.
- **Confess the sin** Specifically calling out the sin privately on a regular basis is important, but so is confessing it to others. When we have sinned against a person or group of people, we may need to approach them and put our confession into words.
- **Ask for forgiveness** Next, we need to ask for forgiveness from those we or others have sinned against. We therefore need to ask this from both the Lord and the person or people concerned. We have to recognize, however, that, depending on the issue, the person or people may not be ready to forgive us. Our confession does not automatically mean that the other or others will be ready to forgive. If we ask for forgiveness and it is not given, then

at least we know that we are forgiven by God. We are all broken people, so we need to do what we can, but without forcing anyone to respond in the way we want them to.

- **Turn away from sin** At this point, we will have confessed our sin and now we need to choose not to repeat the sin again. That means we need to turn our backs on our old self and walk away. This has to be done with sincerity and often we need to do it in a strategic way. If we know that we have a problem with a specific sin, then we need to be practical and put plans in place to ensure we do not go there again. We can't be half-hearted about our sin. As alcoholics recognize, one is always too many and 1,000 is never enough.
- **Put right the wrong** Where possible, true repentance involves us rectifying what we have done wrong, making good, correcting a mistake. Making a positive change is a part of the repentance process. We need to think about what we can do to put things right once more.

Tip We can use a set prayer to help us confess our sin. Many Christian traditions have liturgies that can help us do this. Using such a liturgy can form part of a regular rhythm of confession, which can help us to face up to our sin.

Identificational repentance

In Nehemiah 1.6–7, the prophet confesses 'the sins *we* Israelites, including myself and my father's family, have committed against you'.

Identificational repentance is not as familiar or practised as much as the kind of personal repentance we are all familiar with. Cris has unpacked the concept for us in this chapter so that we can add it to our prayer lives, but perhaps a couple of modern-day, inspirational stories can help to illustrate the power of this form of repentance.

Pastor Bob Fox, in his chapter 'Identificational repentance', from his book *Healing America's DNA* (CreateSpace Independent

Publishing Platform, 2004, also available online, Extra, 19 March 2020, at: <https://bobfox.org/identificational-repentance>), tells the following story.

It was a strange sight. On a warm Argentinian day in 1997, one hundred young Chinese adults from Hong Kong crowded on to the speaker's platform in Buenos Aires, the capital, while a Japanese man in his sixties began to apologize to them . . .

As the older Japanese man began to repent for the atrocities committed against Chinese people by Japan's military in WWII, the room became very silent. Then the Chinese people began to weep silently. Orientals are not prone to public displays of emotion. It seemed like a dam of pent-up emotion broke as the Japanese man continued to humbly and emotionally ask them to forgive his nation for those wartime sins. Soon, the soft sounds of sobbing turned into a loud gusher of uncontrolled wailing in the Chinese group! What made this scene even more amazing is that none of them had actually participated in WWII. None of the Chinese there had even been alive during that war. They were simply representing their respective nations in this time of reconciliation for the sins of a former generation.

Toward the end, a member of the Chinese group, on behalf of the Chinese people, accepted the apologies of the Japanese man who had repented on behalf of Japan. Now it was the Japanese man's turn to cry. Everyone was deeply touched. God was among us in a very special way to heal the hearts of those from both nations.

Finally, it was over. Everyone could tell that a great emotional catharsis had taken place. The representatives from both nations felt much more love for each other. They had experienced emotional healing together as they represented each of their nations in this act of repentance.

Here is another example.

> When Ed Silvoso, the Argentinian evangelist, visited the UK
> in the 1990s he asked for cities to twin as a demonstration of
> unity. This was quite a challenge as church unity movements
> didn't really exist. Liverpool and Manchester responded and a
> joint prayer meeting was held. God began to reveal aspects of
> bitterness which existed between the two cities. This included
> football rivalry. Folks attending the meeting had brought their
> football scarves to lay down at the foot of the cross as an act of
> prayer. As the prayers of repentance about the rivalry began,
> people started to bless the other team and swap scarves.
> Tears flowed as God revealed hatred and bitterness between
> the two cities. Many say that this was the start of the cities of
> Manchester and Liverpool working together. This led to the
> Christian Mission Festival Manchester in 2003 and a similar
> mission, Merseyfest, in 2005. Each city used a similar model
> and shared best practice. More than 25,000 people attended
> Merseyfest each day!

Where to start with confession and repentence

Having decided to identify sins and confess them, as individual
Christians and within the whole body of Christ, we might need
some help to work out a framework for thinking about the various
kinds of sins to get started. Here is a grid that is very useful for
doing exactly that, enabling us to gather together issues that need to
be brought into the light. The headings in each of the boxes can be
read in any way you like; they are simply there to get you thinking
and organizing those thoughts in such a way that you can then take
a step towards confession. Name issues, topics, problems, sinfulness
that come to mind in each of the areas that we, as the Church, need
to confess, repent of and ask forgiveness for.

Church and denominational	The outsider
Sanctity of life	Family life
Gender	Class
Race and nationality	Additional needs and disabilities
Truthfulness	Human sexuality
Climate and creation care	Public and private behaviour
Selfishness	Values
Historical issues	Injustice
Systemic issues*	Other

* A 'systemic issue' is one that has come about as a result of structural and inherent problems in an overall system or organization, rather than owing to specific, individual, isolated influences.

Where to start with identificational repentance

With this type of repentance specifically, it might be helpful to remember the following.

- **Research your area**   This should be done with others, not on your own.
  - Do some research (sometimes called spiritual mapping) into the history of your town/city/country. One way to do this is to print out or draw a large map of your area. On the map, mark or write locations that, historically, have had issues or are known spiritual strongholds.
  - Some aspects you might want to explore are the origins of your area. What are some of the founding principles of or historical phenomena that have occurred in your area that it would be good to be aware of?
  - Are there, or have there been, any stoppers to the gospel? What are the prevalent sins or recurring sins affecting your community? These might include racism, sectarianism, alcoholism, family breakdown, materialism, suicide or a whole host of other possible issues.
  - It is worth looking at what has happened in your area in the past. Has there been a move of God, a revival or a season of fruitfulness? If so, you can use this to pray for more for today. Try thanking God for what was experienced in the area before and ask God for a new season of this right now. Is there a passage of Scripture or a prophetic picture that God has given before or is wanting to give right now for your area?
  - What is it that God is saying to you in what you find out about your people, city or area? This should serve as a foundation for all your prayers about them. You might like to take some time simply to listen to God to find out about what is happening spiritually regarding your local community.

- **Unity is powerful** When we pray together with others, our prayers are magnified. As the old saying goes, a burden shared is a burden halved. Share your burden and help to carry those of others. Remember, Jesus told us, 'Again, truly I tell you that if two of you on earth agree about anything they ask for, it will be done for them by my Father in heaven. For where two or three gather in my name, there am I with them' (Matthew 18.19–20).
- **The word 'Amen' means 'I agree'** We add weight to a prayer by saying the word 'Amen'.
- **In prayer, ask God to break down denominational barriers** in your neighbourhood.
- **Identify common ground** and things that, as Christians, you can agree about and begin to pray about those things.
- **Repent** of any areas of disunity.
- **Pray** a blessing over someone else's church or do a prayer walk around local churches, stopping at each one to pray a prayer of blessing.
- **Volunteer** for a project that has volunteers who come from different churches, denominations or even faiths.

From research to prayer

In the previous pages we have been exploring ways in which we can gather the information we need to find sins that we can confess and repent.

Like any form of prayer, it can be hard to structure and phrase confession and repentance. Certainly, regular prayer meetings held in churches are not well attended, and many Christians find prayer difficult or boring. However, there are some creative ideas for prayer that can make it more tangible and improve our prayer lives, whether we are praying individually or corporately. It is not always easy to confess our shortcomings and it is even harder to do so when we don't feel personally responsible for things we're confessing that were done in our name or happened at some time in the past. Hopefully, though, some of the ideas listed below will spark something and interest or inspire your private prayers as well as those said in church.

- **Shout it out**   Like many areas of prayer, an easy way to confess in a group with others is to have someone read out the list of issues that need to be confessed. Such a list might have been generated by completing the grid on page 46. As someone reads out a few of the issues, the congregation can then respond together, 'We are sorry.' Doing this creates a lightly liturgical framework to the confessions.
- **Take photos of things that inspire you to pray**   They can serve as reminders of things to be thankful for, but can also help us to confess their opposites. For example, a photograph of a flower can make us grateful for God's nature, but it can also call us to confess the harm that we humans have done to the planet.
- **Use a newspaper or online news website**   Ask God to focus your attention on a specific story that needs our prayers.
- **Go for a prayer walk and pray over what you see and hear**   You might hear a siren and pray for the emergency services, for example.
- **Use a length of string with some pegs to display cards showing things or people to pray for at your church**   You could all take one card and bring a card to add to the string.
  Pray over a map of your community, town or city   Thank God for all he has done in your area, and ask forgiveness for neglect or historical oppression, for example, as an act of identificational repentance.
- **Write your prayer on a stone**   Write things you want to confess and repent of and then throw the stone or stones into the river, sea or a lake.
- **Write your prayers down on pieces of paper**   Place the prayers inside balloons, then pump them up and release them.

- **Set up a prayer room, with various stations in it to visit** Be creative. One prayer room had a paddling pool in it with plastic ducks that had prophetic words stuck to them. Go fishing! You could add a wailing wall or a lament station. In a post-COVID world, we want to provide people with an outlet for their pain and a place to grieve. Encourage people to write down the names of lost loved ones and pin them to a lament station.
- **Keep a list of the names of people you are praying for and their prayer requests** You can do this individually or in a home group, for example. When prayers are answered, it will inspire you as well as the subjects of the prayers.

Helpful resources

- Books:
  - Martin Scott (2004) *Gaining Ground* (Lancaster: Sovereign World)
  - John Dawson (1994) *Healing America's Wounds* (Ada, MI: Baker)
  - Roger Mitchell and Brian Mills (1999) *Sins of the Fathers* (Lancaster: Sovereign World)
  - Ed Silvoso (2017) *Ekklesia* (Ada, MI: Chosen, Baker)
- The New Gen Church in Sidcup has regularly used the ideas given on its website (at: <www.larksidcup.com>) at its summer festival, Lark in the Park. Maybe you will find something there that inspires you.

Part 2
RENEW

In the month of Nisan in the twentieth year of King Artaxerxes, when wine was brought for him, I took the wine and gave it to the king. I had not been sad in his presence before, so the king asked me, 'Why does your face look so sad when you are not ill? This can be nothing but sadness of heart.'

I was very much afraid, but I said to the king, 'May the king live for ever! Why should my face not look sad when the city where my ancestors are buried lies in ruins, and its gates have been destroyed by fire?'

The king said to me, 'What is it you want?'
(Nehemiah 2.1–4)

5

Reality check: vision and focus

We need to ask ourselves some stark questions: Have we lost our way? Do our churches behave like Jesus? Is the Church heading in the same direction that the Spirit is blowing or are we way off track?

To move from confession and fasting on to the next step of vision and focus, we should first recognize that we have lost focus. We have taken our eyes off that which needs our attention and allowed ourselves to be distracted by secondary things. How often is church attendance, bums on seats, the litmus test for a church's success? We focus on what those outside the Church see as success rather than staying true to the vision of honouring Jesus and living for him.

It could be said that we have become so determined on succeeding in the running of our services to increase attendance that we have failed to come back to Jesus and check in with his plan for the Church. The words of Amos could be truer now than ever:

I hate, I despise your religious festivals;
    your assemblies are a stench to me.
Even though you bring me burnt offerings and grain offerings,
    I will not accept them.
Though you bring choice fellowship offerings,
    I will have no regard for them.
Away with the noise of your songs!
    I will not listen to the music of your harps.
But let justice roll on like a river,
    righteousness like a never-failing stream!
(Amos 5.21–24)

Our vision has become one of church maintenance and the running of programmes rather than fulfilling the call of God to go into the world and make disciples. That has been forgotten. The life of a Christian community should centre on justice and righteousness and less on the practicalities of how worship is done. For many of us, our buildings, programmes and history have become the ball-and-chains to our faith. Long gone is 'simply living for Jesus in the everyday'. Our lives are now filled with meetings, boards and sub-committees.

I'm being a little facetious in a way, but simply want to make the point that we need to shift our focus away from these things and centre it on Jesus, his mission and ministry in the world. Being completely honest, when did you last ask Jesus how you could help? Have you ever offered to partner with him to see his work in the world fulfilled? The vision has to be all about Jesus and nothing else, so we are 'fixing our eyes on Jesus, the pioneer and perfecter of faith' (Hebrews 12.2a).

Scripture demonstrates the importance of having a clear vision. As it says in Proverbs 29.18, 'Where there is no revelation, people cast off restraint'. The Church has been perishing for a while. We see churches struggling everywhere and it is time to turn things around by having a clear vision and focus.

I was talking with a pastor friend a few years ago about his church. It's a church that has been having difficulties for a while. I cautiously asked him why things had been hard, why he thought that the church was in decline and what he felt needed to happen. His response was interesting. It was the church across the road's fault; it had taken all the best people in the neighbourhood. It was the fault with the building, as it wasn't in good condition. He also blamed the congregation for not liking his teaching because he was too 'truthful'. It was even the assistant pastor's fault for not being more energetic and engaging. We prayed together. We offered love and encouragement for the work that they were doing there.

About a year later, I met a lady who had been a member of my friend's church. She shared how it had once been a fantastic church.

She expressed how sad she was that it was no longer full and even told me why she had left the church. Funnily enough, she never mentioned the building, the energy of the assistant pastor or even the church across the road. Her answer was simple: there was no vision and purpose for the church. The church lacked identity, drive and direction apart from the Sunday service.

She left the church because of the lack of vision.

Fresh vision and renewed focus on the mission of Jesus are what every church needs. In each of our neighbourhoods, if we want to be a church that exists for Jesus and not ourselves, we must define, plan and implement our vision. If we want our church to be a comfortable place for Christians, then vision isn't necessary because we are already content in our bubble. However, if we want to see our church as the bride of Christ, called to reach the lost, transform lives and restore our communities, well, we must set that as our a vision. Not only must we have a renewed vision, we also need a strategy to turn it into reality. The famous saying often attributed to business management guru Peter Drucker is true: 'Culture eats strategy for breakfast', but the lack of a strategy will do the same. It's the two together, vision and strategy, that are necessary to becoming the vibrant, loving, welcoming, life-giving church we are called to be.

Where strategy and vision intersect, we find action.

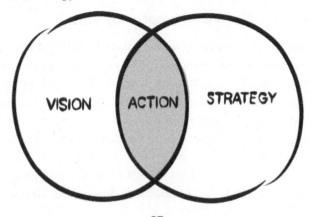

Is there a difference between vision and strategy? Absolutely there is!

A clear vision is about where you want to go, what you want to become, what you want to accomplish. A strategy will help you to get there.

Revolution

A revolution is future-facing; it is powered by a vision that can be seen on the horizon. Anything other than a revolution is nothing more than a church day out. If the vision for the Church could be accomplished simply by hard work, maybe we are missing something. If our vision could be financed by our present financial capacity, maybe we are missing something. If our vision could be accomplished in five to ten years if we worked hard enough, then we are certainly missing something. The vision for the future of the Church should scare you. If it doesn't, is it really a revolutionary vision? It should bring us to our knees, wondering how we will ever achieve it.

In the same breath, it should excite us to see how Jesus will deliver it.

Our vision, not *your* vision

A vision for your church should be a shared vision and not simply the vision of the lead pastor, priest or vicar. This requires that it originate from the leadership but be adopted, owned together and understood by the congregation. Time and time again, we see churches where the leadership team has a fantastic and exciting vision. This might trickle down to the elders or deacons, but then stops there. Hear me now, if the vision isn't embraced and owned by the congregation, it will not become a reality. If it is not going to have an impact on the wider church, if these others are not going to own it, too, it won't get off the ground. In fact, most likely, it will bring about conflict or be received with apathy at best.

Sadly, many church leaders believe that simply communicating the vision in a sermon will lead to it becoming a shared vision. Note: 'hearing' and 'owning' are two very different things. Just because I hear the words spoken about a vision doesn't mean that I want, or have a desire, to make it a reality.

Your vision is not necessarily my vision.

Our vision, though, is our vision.

Inspiring and challenging

When casting the vision for your church, it needs to inspire people to embrace it. It needs to leave them desperate to play their part and be challenging enough that they can see themselves growing into it. The vision needs to leave people wanting to find out more, get involved and get others involved.

If you are a church leader reading this, you might need to think about how you yourself inspire people. Have you ever been invited on a day trip only to find out that where you're going sounds rubbish and you're not remotely interested? You committed yourself before you knew what the destination was and now you feel obliged to support that friend rather than really want to be on the journey. Well . . . that is how many people in our congregations feel. If you are likeable and inspiring, if you make people feel good, then they might come because of your leadership. If your personality doesn't stand out in the crowd and the destination sounds dull, then don't be surprised if people drift off and find better things to do.

A church leader must lead people into a bigger and better future, provide an inspiring, motivating, challenging, memorable and unique picture of where the church is headed. The best leaders engage their people in the process of creating a shared vision. We have to ask ourselves, 'Is our vision big enough and bold enough?', while at the same time achievable, with God's help, and relevant enough to engage those in your church?

Before going any further, let me just clarify what we mean by 'achievable'. Our vision needs to be kingdom big but also based in reality. If the vision is to be the first church to plant a congregation on the dark side of the moon, we have to ask, 'Is this going to be a realistic possibility with the resources we have?' Our vision has to make sense and be possible from a practical point of view, while at the same time be big enough that only God could help us pull it off. That said, anyone want to plant a church with me on the dark side of the moon?

If you aren't a church leader or a part of any formal leadership team, you don't get out of any of this work. The challenge to you is, how are you going to help the leadership team in this task? What part can you play? How can you encourage others? How can you bring out the best in your leaders?

Our vision must shape our strategy

Your church's vision must inform all long-term decisions for that church. The vision needs to shape how decisions are made, who is employed, how services are run, as well as who you might partner with. The vision has to influence every level of your church's life. If it doesn't, it is not a vision – it is a strapline. A church can adopt a vision, but if it is not guiding each and every decision in terms of personnel and staffing, programmes and courses, funding and finance, then it's a toothless tiger.

What follows might require difficult, even painful, decisions to be made. Nehemiah shows us that this was true for his vision, too, and means it holds up as an inspirational example for us today. Tough conversations are part and parcel of establishing the church's vision and seeing it through to becoming a reality. To do this we need to be SMART . . .

S

Specific | Make your goals specific and narrow for more effective planning

M

Measurable | Define what evidence will prove you're making progress and re-evaluate when necessary.

A

Attainable | Make sure your goal is achievable but also bold.

R

Relevant | Your goals should align with your values and vision.

T

Time-bound | Set realistic, ambitious end dates to prioritize each task and maintain motivation.

The process of setting SMART goals is integral to establishing the vision as it will help to:

- establish clear intentions – broad or vague ideas will be weeded out;
- provide a gauge for the direction and establish markers to check progress en route to the goals set;
- offer sensible aims that are realistic and achievable;
- remove unnecessary, unhelpful or irrelevant tasks that often can be distracting;
- establish an achievable timeline.

Clear and focused

In this chapter, we have established how important it is that our church's vision is clear and focused, with a direct, obtainable strategy. How we will get there, in terms of our relationships with one another, is as important as reaching the final goal. Remember, a vision is nothing without people. One without the other will leave members of your church burnt out and frustrated and could have as damaging an effect as a lack of vision.

How can you see if your church has a vision and a strategy? Is it simply about having something up on the wall?

One of the ways in which we can test our vision is by looking to see if there are any fruits from it. These are the proof that there is a vision and plan of action in place and they are working.

Do you see any fruits from your church's vision? If the answer is 'No', then you might need to talk with people to find out why. Does the vision need to be made clearer, easier to understand or act on? If people understand what the vision looks like in reality, they are much more likely to live it out and it is then that you will see it bear fruit.

6

Nehemiah 2: casting a new vision

I went to Jerusalem, and after staying there three days I set out
during the night with a few others. I had not told anyone what
my God had put in my heart to do for Jerusalem. There were
no mounts with me except the one I was riding on.

By night I went out through the Valley Gate towards the Jackal
Well and the Dung Gate, examining the walls of Jerusalem,
which had been broken down, and its gates, which had been destroyed by fire. Then I moved on towards the Fountain Gate and
the King's Pool, but there was not enough room for my mount
to get through; so I went up the valley by night, examining the
wall. Finally, I turned back and re-entered through the Valley
Gate. The officials did not know where I had gone or what I was
doing, because as yet I had said nothing to the Jews or the priests
or nobles or officials or any others who would be doing the work.

Then I said to them, 'You see the trouble we are in: Jerusalem
lies in ruins, and its gates have been burned with fire. Come,
let us rebuild the wall of Jerusalem, and we will no longer be in
disgrace.' I also told them about the gracious hand of my God
on me and what the king had said to me.
(Nehemiah 2.11–18)

Assessing needs and casting the vision

As we continue to study the book of Nehemiah, chapter 2 offers a
helpful structure for identifying the needs we wish to address and
casting the vision. Doing this is necessary not only for our churches
but also for our personal lives.

It is an inborn human characteristic to want to leave a mark to show for our time on earth. As Richard Leider put it in an interview for *Fast Company* magazine (Alan M. Webber, 'Are you deciding on purpost (extended interview), 31 January 1998, at: <www.fast company. com/33161/are-you-deciding-purpose-extended-interview>):

> Everyone wants to leave behind some kind of legacy, some kind of personal mark. It doesn't have to be great or magnificent. But human beings know that at one level, we each have a [sic] own unique thumbprint, and we all want to leave that print behind for others to see that we've been here.

As Christians, this takes the form of wanting to make a positive difference and be part of something bigger than ourselves. Often people think that they don't have much to offer, but the reality is everyone can be – and, indeed is – involved in changing the world. Each cog is needed to make the machinery work.

Each person also needs to know what to focus on and what to do so that all are working fruitfully within the whole. Without a focus we can float from one thing to another to another, a bit aimlessly, and end up not driving things forwards in a productive way.

You were born with a part to play . . . Do you know what it is yet?

Psychologists have identified three desires that are common to every person on the planet. They are to:

- connect to the creative spirit;
- express our gifts and talents;
- know that our lives matter.

Wanting to make sure that we leave the world a better place because we were in it, then, is a great human desire, but how do we go about doing that?

There is no one, clear, step-by-step process. Each of us is unique, so we each walk a slightly different path through life. Much like our thumbprints, therefore, no two journeys are exactly the same.

Similarly, each church is unique and so we need to check in regularly with one another to ensure that we stay on course as we work towards achieving the vision and maintain our focus. We should ask, 'Is this still what we are meant to be doing? Are we in line with what God wants us to do in our community?' Each period of time may require a different focus, as we navigate difficult terrain, for example.

To ensure also, more importantly, that we stay within God's will for us, we must always review and reassess. For churches, this process often happens when there are leadership changes or a cultural shift. Such events reveal opportunities to develop and re-engage. In a post-COVID world, for example, the Church recognizes that the walls which once delineated 'church' have now moved. We think differently and understand the world in other ways and this has consequences for reforming the Church.

Nehemiah's people had been removed from the structures and community of old Jerusalem so, as they returned from exile, they had to work out methodically how, where and when to rebuild. In a similar way, during the pandemic we were 'exiled', not able to go inside the walls of our churches. We could gather only in small groups in our homes, but used technology in a way that we had not really considered before. After an extended period away from the gathered Church, we return with the knowledge that, like Nehemiah, we aren't the same people we were. We have experienced too much, grown in new ways and carry a deep grief for both people and things that have been lost. As a result, we are left with some important decisions. Where do we go from here? What do we rebuild? Our thinking is certainly not focused on buildings; it is focused on people.

Nehemiah doesn't give us a step-by-step process. Nor is there a manual. What we do get from Nehemiah is his journey, which can help us to work out our next steps.

Nehemiah: visionary, prophet and builder

Moving deeper into the book of Nehemiah, we realize a few things about the character of the man. Nehemiah was incredibly practical; he was detail-orientated while at the same time being a big-picture prophet. Nehemiah saw what could be done. He could picture in his mind not only how the city would look but also how it would function. Later in the book of Nehemiah, we see how he challenged the poverty people were suffering (chapter 5), the centrality of Scripture (chapter 8) and the distinctiveness of the people (chapter 10).

Nehemiah was a builder, prophet and pastor.

As we work out the vision for the future of our local churches and the Church as a whole, the role played by the prophets is central. Unless we listen to the prophets, we will end up creating things that fulfil human needs rather than work towards the bigger vision of the kingdom.

Walter Brueggemann, in *The Prophetic Imagination* (Fortress, 2001), writes about the role of the prophets as having two aspects. The first is to evoke grief and the second is to create amazement. Grief for what has been lost, and amazement for the new worlds that are possible. (If you haven't read Walter Brueggemann's book, we would encourage you to do so.) Brueggemann also writes that the 'task of prophetic ministry is to nurture, nourish, and evoke a consciousness and perception alternative to the consciousness and perception of the dominant culture around us'. In other words, prophets and vision casters point people beyond their own imaginations towards a vision that is so big only God can pull it off. As humans, we can come up with visions that fit our abilities or the accepted culture around us, but prophets can lift our eyes above the prevailing culture to the bigger vision of the kingdom found through and in the resurrection. This is what Nehemiah does for us in the next part of the story. As Brueggemann goes on to write in his book:

The prophet engages in futuring fantasy. The prophet does not ask if the vision can be implemented, for questions of implementation are of no consequence until the vision can be imagined. The imagination must come before the implementation. Our culture is competent to implement almost anything and to imagine almost nothing. The same royal consciousness that makes it possible to implement anything and everything is the one that shrinks imagination because imagination is a danger. Thus, every totalitarian regime is frightened of the artist. It is the vocation of the prophet to keep alive the ministry of imagination, to keep on conjuring and proposing future alternatives to the single one the king wants to urge as the only thinkable one.

Most of us simply aren't prophets. We have neither the skills nor the imagination required. We can't all be like Nehemiah. Many of us need to hear from him and the other prophets and visionaries to then know how we can play our part in helping to make the vision a reality.

It's amazing to think that Nehemiah had such a unique collection of gifts, being able to see both the detail and the big picture. This isn't the case for so many of us. Knowing who we are and what we can bring to the table is important. If you are a prophet, though, if you see the big picture, if you sense and see the vision God is calling the Church to, then be liberated to practise your gift, be that person. If, however, you are a detail-focused person or someone who is a doer, then be set free to be that person. Enjoy being the person you are with your own gifts. As we read through the book of Nehemiah, we can think that we should all be like Nehemiah, but this isn't the case.

Often prophets of today are left on the fringes. They can be uncomfortable to be around and challenge us in ways that we simply don't want. Please bear in mind the warning that, if we don't listen to the prophets in our midst, we will miss what God is doing and what God is wanting. History has shown us that when prophets are cast aside, ignored by those in power, then the lives of disciples and followers of Jesus are left wanting.

Nehemiah, prayer and focus

Then I prayed to the God of heaven, and I answered the king.
(Nehemiah 2.4–5)

To renew our focus, we need to start from a place of prayer. In prayer we come to know the mind of God. If we look at the life of Jesus, we can see his rhythm of retreating and then advancing. Jesus often retreated to a quiet place right before his clear focus then drove him to show his signs and wonders.

But Jesus often withdrew to lonely places and prayed.
(Luke 5.16)

After this, Jesus healed a paralysed man.

Very early in the morning, while it was still dark, Jesus got up, left the house and went off to a solitary place, where he prayed.
(Mark 1.35)

Jesus then healed a man of a skin disease.

To advance into the mission of God, Nehemiah and Jesus both spent time in prayer and fasting, and we must do the same. To grab the vision and mission with the full encouragement of God, we need to be praying and fasting first.

The passage from Nehemiah at the beginning of this chapter demonstrates how he came to have and was now following his leadership vision: it was because of 'what my God . . . put in my heart' (2.12). That is, he took the time to listen to God's heart and desires. How often do we practise listening? When we set aside time to hear God, his leadership begins. God's influence begins to weave through our lives. A Christian leader is nothing more than a disciple who has influence. Yes, there is 'calling', when God specifically draws certain people into leadership, but for most of us, the highest calling is to be a disciple of Jesus who has a positive and godly influence in the world and the lives of others. Each disciple can, therefore, be someone of influence . . . can give leadership.

Doing what's in front of us

Your availability is far more important to God than your capability. We get these things really mixed up in our minds. We are full of excuses as to why now isn't the right time and why we aren't the ones for the task. Simply, again, God isn't looking for our capability, simply our availability.

> I was cupbearer to the king.
> (Nehemiah 1.11)

As we look through the book of Nehemiah, we see a man who lived his life with a focus that only became clear later in life. As we see here, he was a cup bearer to the king. This line is the most helpful for many of us. We can live our lives paralysed by not knowing what our focus is or what God wants for us so, in this state, we do nothing. Nehemiah's story gives us permission to keep doing what is directly in front of us until we understand what our place is in the bigger picture. Also, we can be liberated by the role that Nehemiah held at court. Yes, it was a position of high standing, but it was also a simple position. Nehemiah was like the tea boy! We think that it is the great people, interesting people, educated people, wealthy people who do great things, but Nehemiah demonstrated that even a tea boy can be called to do great things.

69

Nehemiah was . . .

not a political adviser
not a financial adviser
not a military adviser
not a rule maker
not a decision maker . . .

Nehemiah was the tea boy.

A cup bearer, historically, was an officer of high rank in the royal courts whose duty it was to pour and serve the drinks at the royal table. Owing to the constant fear of plots and intrigues (such as poisoning), a person must have been regarded as thoroughly trust-worthy to be appointed to this position.

It may also be that the thing right in front of us is the place God wants us to focus on and serve. We can often be looking to the future, to the next new thing, while the place we are right now is the right place for us to be at this time. Nehemiah served the king and that was the right place for him to be until God called him.

In this, Nehemiah showed that availability is far more important to God than capability. Training, wealth and talents are wonderful, and we should be grateful for them, but our availability to God is key. Sadly, our training, wealth and talents can, in fact, stop us from truly being available to God, emotionally or spiritually.

There is nothing to indicate how old Nehemiah was when he left the court of King Artaxerxes in Susa. This is significant for many of us. We think that our whole lives need to be lived for a powerful vision and mission, but Nehemiah served God just as much while in exile as he did when he moved to Jerusalem. We must also note that Nehemiah returned to that 'normal' life once the city had been rebuilt. That is, after 12 years as governor, during which time he ruled with justice and righteousness, he returned to the king in Susa. Most of Nehemiah's life, then, was normal rather than spent doing the dynamic work of building walls and constructing a city. Like us, therefore, Nehemiah was working in a normal world, loving an amazing God, serving him by doing what was right in front of him with justice and righteousness. He was an average person. Then God called him out of that life.

If nothing else, we learn from Nehemiah the importance of making our Monday-to-Saturday life point towards God. We need to build up our reputations as good people so that when that day comes and God calls us to do something, we can step into that.

Nehemiah does research

I went to Jerusalem, and after staying there three days I set out during the night with a few others. I had not told anyone what my God had put in my heart to do for Jerusalem. There were no mounts with me except the one I was riding on.
(Nehemiah 2.11–12)

Nehemiah had been told about the problems in Jerusalem, so he knew from others that the walls needed to be rebuilt, but he didn't have the full picture. Before Nehemiah could start to work out his vision and the focus of the work required, he needed to understand the scope and details of the problem. That could only be done by leaving the court and seeing with his own eyes the reality of the situation. Once he had done that and talked with the people there, then he could start to work on solutions. Until that point everything was purely hypothetical. Physically looking at the site allowed Nehemiah to understand fully the issues at hand but it also allowed him to work out what could be salvaged, what was missing and what new resources would be needed.

Then I [Nehemiah] said to them, 'You see the trouble we are in: Jerusalem lies in ruins, and its gates have been burned with

fire. Come, let us rebuild the wall of Jerusalem, and we will no
longer be in disgrace.'
(Nehemiah 2.17)

Nehemiah did not research the situation alone; he collaborated
with others. Nehemiah knew that if others were to catch the vision,
they would need to join him in coming to understand the problem.
That way, they would take ownership of it too. Nehemiah brought
in others who he knew were reliable to be a part of the vision and
mission. This small group joined him in understanding the scale of
the problem and in finding the solution.

The research element of Nehemiah's journey is massively significant. If you have ever had a problem in your workplace, community
or church, you will know from your own experience that including
people in the problem immediately makes them part of the solution.
They are then 'onside' and sometimes become even more passionate
than you!

When God calls us and gives us a focus and vision, before we
act, we must first fully investigate what he is calling us to do. This
includes looking into the history, culture and issues involved. Being
called gives us authority to do the thing, but being prepared before
taking action honours that calling. Jesus said, 'Don't begin until
you count the cost. For who would begin construction of a building
without first calculating the cost to see if there is enough money to
finish it?' (Luke 14.28, NLT). Just like a builder, we need to get the
facts straight and fully understand the issues to do a good job. There
are always those who want to skip this part and push to get straight
to solving the problem. They are the doers and God calls them, too,
but preparation is a necessary part of the process and must take
precedence. The wisdom Nehemiah models for us is the importance
of taking time to understand, evaluate and set a vision on firm foundations with others.

Nehemiah's timing is right

When, like Nehemiah, we are looking at the rubble around us, we might ask ourselves not only what the problem is but also is this the time to solve it?

There are many problems that we *can* solve, but they should only be solved when the time is right. Nehemiah heard about the problem, but was he called to solve the problem in that moment? Was he even the right person for that moment? Nehemiah could have been prompted by God to simply pray for the issue because God had someone else in mind for the task. Indeed, the walls of Jerusalem had been in ruins for many years, so why was then the time to rebuild them?

Discerning the right time is key for everyone. There were a few key elements in Nehemiah's story that we can learn from.

- The strength of Nehemiah's conviction. The passion of his prayer (Nehemiah 1) conveys that he has experienced a divine moment deep inside. He was broken by the news Hanani brought him, which prepared him for being called to resolve that situation. Nehemiah aligned his heart with God's and, as a result, he could envision the devastation in the way that God did, so his heart was broken in the same way as God's. What followed was a deep conviction that he needed to act.
- There was a God-given moment when the king saw Nehemiah's distress and gave him the option to go and be a part of the rebuilding. The king could have ignored Nehemiah's distress, he could have forbidden him to leave, he could have stopped him in any number of ways. The point is, he didn't. That 'open door' was a sign of what was to follow.
- Timing is everything. Nehemiah could have been called and felt a sense of conviction, but if the vision hadn't taken root, then the timing might have been off. The final challenge in discerning whether or not it was the right time was the response of the people to Nehemiah's call when he made it.

In casting the vision, Nehemiah offered an argument for why that was indeed the right time. In chapter 2.18, he said, 'I also told them about the gracious hand of my God on me and what the king had said to me.' Put simply, because God had made a way for it to happen. It had been God's divine hand that had cleared a route for Nehemiah to be in *that* place at *that* moment so *that* vision could become a reality.

Nehemiah shifted his perspective

We can also learn from Nehemiah that, when we are exploring a problem, we need to make sure that we are changing our perspective on it as we do so. Let's look again at how Nehemiah assessed the problem before him:

> By night I went out through the Valley Gate towards the Jackal Well and the Dung Gate, examining the walls of Jerusalem, which had been broken down, and its gates, which had been destroyed by fire. Then I moved on towards the Fountain Gate and the King's Pool, but there was not enough room for my mount to get through; so I went up the valley by night, examining the wall. Finally, I turned back and re-entered through the Valley Gate. (Nehemiah 2.13–15)

Nehemiah thus began by looking at all the details. On his mount he went from the Valley Gate to the south west of the city, south to the Jackal Well, Dung Gate and then round to the Fountain Gate.

Nehemiah was looking at all the details of the wells, gates entranceways and pools. We can imagine Nehemiah checking what bricks were usable, which gates and woodwork needed to be replaced. He was assessing, in great detail, a small section of the southern end of the city, but could not get further at that point as the rubble blocked his way. He then went from assessing the detail

Nehemiah 2: casting a new vision

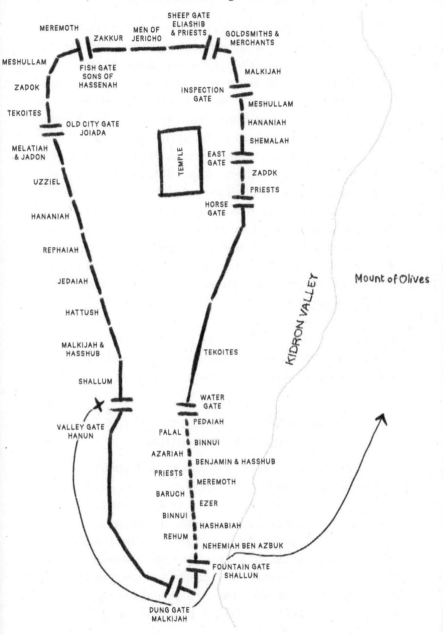

to travelling up and over the valley to look at the city from a distance. Imagine this for a moment. Nehemiah was assessing the damage from across the valley. It was from across the valley, too, that Jesus prayed for the city. It was across the valley that Jesus went to the Garden of Gethsemane. The view of the city from there is as spectacular today as it would have been disappointing then. You can see the city clearly as you head further up the valley ridge.

In this way, Nehemiah assessed the details close to, but then shifted his perspective, looking at the city from a distance, as a big picture. He saw the whole city, the whole problem and the whole need.

Just as Nehemiah needed to change his perspective to gather all the information he needed, we might need to shift our perspective on a problem for the same reason. Looking at any situation close up might not give us what we need to access the prophetic part of our imagination. The prayer here for us, as for Nehemiah, needs to be, 'God, change my perspective.'

Often, when we are too close to a problem, we are unable to see the full picture. We need to step back. Equally, if we *only* look at the big picture, we might not see some necessary details. Nehemiah realized that we need both perspectives, and so do we.

Nehemiah communicated the vision as a solution

Nehemiah knew that the vision he had was a solution to a major problem the people of God were experiencing. The city had been decimated and a massive amount of work needed to be done. Nehemiah also knew that he had to inspire the people to get behind the vision so that they would feel ownership of the task ahead of them. Although Nehemiah had the vision, the ability to complete the task was in the hands of the people, with their unique gifts and talents. Nehemiah was under no illusion that things could go wrong. The people of Jerusalem could have taken against him as an outsider and run him out of town. They could have challenged him, saying, 'What do you know, you have only been here a few days?' or, 'Who do you think you are?' The people could have not accepted his leadership, laughed at the size of the problem and decided to simply accept things as they were.

In Nehemiah 2, we have a great lesson in how to communicate your vision to people, how to influence them and secure their involvement:

> Then I [Nehemiah] said to them, 'You see the trouble we are in: Jerusalem lies in ruins, and its gates have been burned with fire. Come, let us rebuild the wall of Jerusalem, and we will no longer be in disgrace.' I also told them about the gracious hand of my God on me and what the king had said to me.
> They replied, 'Let us start rebuilding.' So they began this good work.
> (Nehemiah 2.17–18)

Nehemiah achieved this by communicating the vision in four steps. He set out the:

- problem: 'You see the trouble we are in';
- solution: 'Come, let us rebuild the wall';
- reason for actioning the solution: 'we will no longer be in disgrace';
- timing: 'I also told them about the gracious hand of my God on me.'

Which direction to take?

Backwards

The vision Nehemiah offered the people was an honourable one. It was responding to the needs of the city, to bring back its security, community and pride. For Nehemiah, this vision was solid, but it is not the right solution for us today. This is where we part ways from Nehemiah.

Nehemiah was building backwards. The plan was to rebuild the city so that it would be just like it had been in the golden era the people of God remembered. Just like the good old days. The danger with such sentimentality is that it can lead us astray. It is also the easier option. For the people rebuilding Jerusalem, it was certainly easier and they had fond memories they wanted to go back to. They did not want to build forwards, towards change.

We see this ourselves in the Church today. When a church leader suggests change, it is often met with the hardline response, 'We don't do change.'

Like the people of Jerusalem, we talk about getting back to the good old days, when churches had choirs, the members of the leadership team dressed like leaders and the seats were pews. There is nothing wrong with this; it is in our nature to be sentimental. The Church, however, is not ours, it is God's and we must again check ourselves and ask what God wants us to do.

Forwards

God's plans are always to build and move forwards. God loves the new thing. Isaiah talked about this: 'See I am doing a new thing! Now it springs up; do you not perceive it?' (43.19). It was during this period that the prophet Zechariah spoke to the people of God about what was to be Nehemiah's building project, around 150 years earlier:

> While the angel who was speaking to me was leaving, another angel came to meet him and said to him: 'Run, tell that young man, "Jerusalem will be a city without walls because of the great number of people and animals in it. And I myself will be a wall of fire around it," declares the LORD, "and I will be its glory within."'
> (Zechariah 2.3–5)

The vision, therefore, was always to have a city for God without walls, of no division, where all people would come and be with him.

God wanted to build a radical city, where people of every tribe and nation would come in and not be held back from him. God's city is a welcome, diverse, unboarded place for all people to find a home, safety and salvation. We don't build backwards, we build forwards to create a city where there is no more pain, suffering, tears or death (Revelation 21.4).

The vision

So what is the vision for us today?

Nehemiah lived before Jesus, so his vision could only be formed from what he could imagine. For us, though, the vision is Jesus and the pull of the resurrection is in a forwards direction.

The vision is the renewal of all things and all people.

The vision is a place where all people are equal, loved and saved by Jesus.

The vision is a world that looks more like heaven than hell.

The vision is a place where death is beaten by healthy living and, dare I say, miracles.

The vision is a place where grief is supported and those grieving can be loved and supported.

The vision is no more tears of pain, but turning to tears of joy.

The vision is a place where every person is able to think clear thoughts.

The vision is every disciple living like and as Jesus.

The vision is Jesus over addiction.

The vision is people not living to consume but for the community.

The vision is a place where the prison system is not needed because we can care for people at home.

The vision is radical, welcoming and amazing, because it's Jesus.

Is that even possible? The answer is no, it's not *humanly* possible, but we have God to enable these things to happen. The specific vision for each of our communities needs to be big enough that it scares the pants off of us and only God could pull it off! If you are not asking the questions, 'How do we finance this?', 'How do we resource this?', 'How do we go about realizing your vision, Lord?', then it is probably not big enough.

As we head back to the story of Nehemiah, we do so with *the* Jesus vision at the front of our minds. We don't build backwards, we build forwards, to the new thing that God is doing.

Nehemiah listened to the response

Would Nehemiah have continued if the people had said no? He could have done if his conviction had been strong enough but, in reality, he would have got stuck at some point and the task would have been so much harder. The response from the people in front of him was a clear one, however: 'Let us start rebuilding' (Nehemiah 2.18).

Like Nehemiah, we need those around us to catch the vision and make a commitment to it if we are going to see that vision and focus come to fruition. Nehemiah's building project wasn't a one-man project, it needed the city to respond with a yes.

Leaders will recognize the truth of this, that when God is working with us to set a vision for our communities, we need a committed, focused 'Yes' from our church if we are going to set out to action the task in hand. This clear moment of the community discerning with us where God wills us to work in our local area is what we will need when the criticism comes, and it will come. It gives us a foundation that reinforces what we are doing, as we know that we have the community behind us. For those of us not in specific leadership positions, are we willing to be people who get behind the vision to make it happen and then give support when there is criticism?

This sense of communal alignment with the vision is very important. In the history of the Church, there have been too many people who thought that they heard God tell them to do something, then failed to get other Christians on board; they did not have this moment of discernment and alignment. They then pressed on, without this wider support, believing that they were doing God's will, only to be disappointed with the results. The purpose of listening at the outset is part of the wider process of discerning what God wants us to do. Do others think this is God's idea or just me? Do they agree that this is the time to action it?

Expect criticism and spiritual attack

As Nehemiah found, having a vision and acting on it often lead to criticism and attack, from sometimes obvious but also some more surprising corners. The evil one wants to distract and pull us away from the vision God has given us, which means we need to be ready and aware that this might happen. Please hear me loud and clear when I say this: criticism is not a sign that the vision is wrong. Sometimes there are people who don't get it, people who are stuck or unable to be a part of change for various reasons or a fear of the evil one. There are also some who feel that they have too much to lose if things change – they hold power and don't want to give it up or think there is the potential for power to be gained by others, which they don't want to happen, for example. All of this needs to be taken into account. Nehemiah did so by a shrewd process of discerning God's plan.

Alongside criticism, there is also the possibility that there will be some kind of spiritual attack, sent by the evil one to derail the plan. We see this clearly in Jesus' ministry. It came most obviously when the devil tempted Jesus in the desert (Matthew 4.1–11), but it is also at the root of the critical comments from the Pharisees and other religious leaders. If the devil isn't afraid to try to trip up Jesus, he certainly won't be afraid to go for you.

The line between criticism and spiritual attack can be wafer thin but these two things can also be miles apart. To help you work out which any one instance is, you will need the spiritual gift of discernment and the counsel of the saints. Remember, if what you are facing is a spiritual attack, it will be a battle. Equally, not every criticism comes from Satan. Sometimes it's just the result of human judgement. Being able to step back and work out what is going on is vital. That is why having good, prayerful and wise people around us is so important. We also have to recognize that some people are yes people because they don't want to let us down. Don't surround yourself with yes people; surround yourself with godly people.

What comes next in Nehemiah's process of casting the vision and stepping out in faith with a clear focus is encouraging for us. It can often feel like we are the only ones under attack, but the reality of community and church life is that attacks are real and present and we will all face attack at some point. In every family, in everyday life, in every local church, in every business big and small, there are troublemakers. They will criticize, they will demotivate, they will discourage you from living out God's vision and focus for your life and your church community. In such situations, we have a choice to make: are we going to engage with them or are we going to respectfully disengage from them? Whatever you do, these troublemakers are to be loved and prayed for, even when we don't feel like it. Remember Romans 12.14.

Nehemiah experienced an attack from troublemakers:

But when Sanballat the Horonite, Tobiah the Ammonite official and Geshem the Arab heard about it, they mocked and ridiculed us. 'What is this you are doing?' they asked. 'Are you rebelling against the king?'

I answered them by saying, 'The God of heaven will give us success. We his servants will start rebuilding, but as for

you, you have no share in Jerusalem or any claim or historic
right to it.'
(Nehemiah 2.19–20)

We, like Nehemiah, have a choice to make. Are we going to listen to
the Sanballats and Tobiahs or are we going to make God the louder
voice? This choice isn't just one leaders need to make but one we all
need to make in our churches.

The attacks Nehemiah endured took a number of forms:

- mockery and sarcasm (Nehemiah 4.2–3);
- anger (Nehemiah 4.5);
- threats and intimidation (Nehemiah 4.8, 11);
- discouragement and exhaustion (Nehemiah 4.10);
- negativity from those on his own side (Nehemiah 4.10);
- fear (Nehemiah 4.14).

All of us, in all areas of church and Christian life, need to apply
this approach to attacks we experience. We all need to be asking,
'Whose voice am I listening to? Am I someone who is contributing
to the vision or being a distraction from it?' Sometimes, despite
being well-intentioned, we are, in fact, being the most unhelpful
person in the room.

Opposition is the price of vision; they go hand in hand. The
evil one wants to derail and stop God's plans. We don't know if
Nehemiah expected criticism right from the start, but he was
certainly prepared for it. His response was always straight to
the point:

When Sanballat the Horonite and Tobiah the Ammonite
official heard about this, they were very much disturbed that
someone had come to promote the welfare of the Israelites.
(Nehemiah 2.10)

Notice here the use of the word 'disturbed'. When a vision is cast, there will always be those who are disturbed because they feel threatened. This word is also interesting as it connects the story of Nehemiah with Jesus' experience. Nehemiah came to restore the city and build up the people of God. He did not do this for his own benefit but for the benefit of the people and to strengthen the city dedicated to *YHVH*, the God of Israel. Fast forward to the birth of Jesus in Matthew 2.3. Jesus, too, came to begin a new restoration project. It wasn't the restoration of walls, however, but the restoration of the relationship between us and God. Jesus came to dismantle the walls that had been built by sin in order to build up this relationship once again.

> When King Herod heard this he was *disturbed*, and all Jerusalem with him.
> (Matthew 2.3, italics added)

In using this word, Matthew reminds us that when Nehemiah came to do God's work, in the city, there were those who were threatened, which disturbed them, and when Jesus came, those in power were again disturbed and did all they could to stop his work. In other words, Nehemiah had to watch for and deal with threats and so did Jesus.

Recognizing a spiritual attack

We have to be careful when we start talking about spiritual attacks. Sometimes it's not an attack, it's just a bad coincidence or a result of natural issues or self-inflicted troubles. I personally have experienced situations in which Christians have made poor decisions and then blamed a spiritual attack as being the reason for things going wrong. Equally, as the book of Nehemiah shows us, when we are doing God's work, there are times when the evil one wants to cause disruptions. How, though, can we tell the difference?

It's harder than you might think. Sometimes the evil one can use our poor decisions against us. We also have to recognize, as Jesus makes clear in John 16.33, that we may well experience spiritual trouble simply because we are Jesus' disciples.

Before going into a bit more detail, it's also important to recognize that there's power available to us in the name of Jesus, the Holy Spirit, God's word and prayer, and we can be confident that Jesus is always with us. He leads the way and has got our backs.

There are various forms of spiritual attack to watch out for.

- The kind that comes from out of nowhere. You don't see it coming and, suddenly, you're sent spinning. Often, an attack isn't due to any obvious or valid reason. Sometimes it comes in the form of infighting. If the evil one can cause God's people to argue about an issue for extended periods of time, he is creating disunity and then the family will no longer be functional.
- Out-of-the blue illness or some other life-threatening event. We know from God's word that the enemy wants nothing more than to 'steal and kill and destroy' (John 10.10).
- Sudden increased temptation or a desire to make really poor choices. As Christians, temptations are a daily struggle. They are also a normal issue when we are recovering from a life of sin or leaving a world that is wanting to draw us away from Jesus. The evil one will also use temptation to take people out of ministry, draw them away from their call and render them incapable. A great example of this occurs in Matthew 4.1–11, when Satan tries to tempt Jesus to divert him from the ministry that he is about to start.
- Feeling overwhelmed by despair, depression, anxiety and fear. Like all the schemes of the evil one, we have to be very clear about the source – depressive thoughts are not always from Satan. We all experience dark days and hard times – it's part of being human – but we also know that these things *can* be used to stop us stepping

up or stepping out into the task ahead. We see this happening in the life of Elijah the prophet. He led the battle against the false idols of Baal and brought glory to God. He was seen as a hero of the faith and greatly honoured, yet, during all this, Elijah also experienced extreme levels of spiritual attack. Elijah ran for his life. In despair and under the shadow of depression, he couldn't think straight. At times it looked like he had forgotten everything that God had done for him and through him. You can read about this in 1 Kings 19. Therefore, though ups and downs in our mental health are a part of our humanness, we need to be aware that this tendency can also be used against us. I have experienced dark seasons of the soul myself, when I have allowed myself to focus on the wrong things.

- The slow work of the evil one in cooling down our faith and drawing us away from God's side. He loves to draw us away from God's word and prayer, slowly leading us to think that we are not in need of God's help. Then, over time, we realize that we have become lukewarm and are no longer fulfilling his call.

What do we need to do?

If you sense that what is happening is possibly a spiritual attack, there are some simple things that you can do quickly. First, you need to let others know of your concerns and ask for their input. Choose carefully who you share these concerns with and ask them to keep this confidential. Do they agree with you? Praying with other Christians and putting on your spiritual armour is another key first step towards breaking the power of the attack:

And pray in the Spirit on all occasions with all kinds of prayers and requests. With this in mind, be alert and always keep on praying for all the Lord's people.
(Ephesians 6.18)

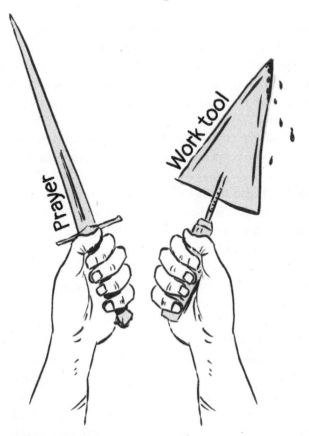

Nehemiah's workers, when they heard about the possibility of attack, prayed and had tools in one hand and swords in the other to defend themselves:

> From that day on, half of my men did the work, while the other half were equipped with spears, shields, bows and armour. The officers posted themselves behind all the people of Judah who were building the wall. Those who carried materials did their work with one hand and held a weapon in the other.
> (Nehemiah 4.16–17)

We must do the same, metaphorically – having the tools for the job in one hand and the gift of prayer and intercession in the other. Also, the workers in Nehemiah going about the business of rebuilding had others defending them with swords and shields, and we also need people around us defending and covering us, but with prayer.

Earlier in the Old Testament there is another description, this time of worship being used to overcome a spiritual attack:

> As they began to sing and praise, the LORD set ambushes against the men of Ammon and Moab and Mount Seir who were invading Judah, and they were defeated.
> (2 Chronicles 20.22)

In our worship, too, we see the work of the evil one lose power against us. Prayer and worship are just what we need to bring down an attack.

The final need of the people of God is to ensure that we do not allow the evil one to establish a foothold in our lives. By committing ourselves to obeying Jesus, we don't allow Satan to use our actions – past or present – against us.

How did Jesus and Nehemiah dismantle the spiritual attack brought by Satan himself and Satan working through people?

- We see that Scripture is always at the heart of dismantling spiritual attack (Matthew 4.7). Jesus quoted it to Satan and Nehemiah had it read to the people by Ezra in Nehemiah 8.
- Both Jesus (in Matthew 5.44) and Nehemiah (Nehemiah 4.4–5) lifted their voices in prayer.
- Both Jesus (Luke 10.18) and Nehemiah (Nehemiah 4.17) also kept their eyes on the enemy. Nehemiah had the people working and carrying a sword at the same time.

Be alert

Many Christians are oblivious to the dangers that come from Satan through spiritual attack, but we must remember these words:

> Be alert and of sober mind. Your enemy the devil prowls around like a roaring lion looking for someone to devour.
> (1 Peter 5.8)

We must also remember that we, as disciples, should go into the world like Nehemiah's workmen did, wearing a spiritual sword. As Ephesians 6.10–20 makes clear, we must also enter the world wearing the full armour of God.

In the face of a spiritual attack, then we must respond in the same way that Nehemiah did, with Scripture and prayer, and by keeping on going with the work, exercising vigilance against the enemy and keeping our focus on the great and awesome God we serve.

7

Yes, but how?

With Debra Green and Paul Weston

Nehemiah's vision was formed *through prayer*, which was *in response* to a need that, ultimately, was brought to his attention by God. Having a vision, and the call related to it, are important and, as Scripture tells us:

> If people can't see what God is doing,
>   they stumble all over themselves;
> But when they attend to what he reveals,
>   they are most blessed.
> (Proverbs 29.18, MSG)

It is in our nature, as humans, to have a vision, goals, something to strive towards. This is just as true today as it was in Nehemiah's time. When he cast his vision, many people chose to follow and play their part. As Cris mentioned in the previous chapter, however, there is always the possibility of opposition to a vision, but most people, as was the case with Nehemiah's, become inspired by it to roll up their sleeves and do their bit.

The vision Nehemiah had was vast. It was for the whole community, a city full of people, all the tribes of Israel, but a vision can be personal too. Both personal and corporate (that is, community, church, organization) goals are important – even vital – for God's kingdom. In this chapter, we are going to look at both personal and corporate visions and how to define, communicate and achieve both.

Discerning your personal vision
Identify your strengths

God helps us to identify our gifts and strengths in a number of ways, including comments from our friends and family, our lived experiences, prophetic words, Scripture and prayer. These can also be determined by looking at our skills, talents and what draws our attention. There are various helpful websites and articles that can help you to do this, including:

- God. Gifts. You. spiritual gifts assessment, at: <https://godgifts you.com/assessment>
- 5 Voices Assessment, at: <https://5voices.com>
- StrengthsFinder, at: <www.gallup.com/cliftonstrengths/en/strengthsfinder.aspx>.

Reflect your values

Your vision should reflect your values. Your values are the fundamental beliefs that guide and motivate your attitudes and actions. Make a list of your core values (such as creativity, kindness, integrity, compassion, generosity).

Apply your skills and vision to an issue

Once God has laid a vision on your heart, do the research – don't assume that you already understand everything about it. Remember how Nehemiah did his research before actioning his vision, by walking around the city, assessing the damage and viewing it from the hillside across the valley to get the full picture. Make sure that you do your research, too, by asking the people in the community what is needed.

Doing this does three very powerful things:

- you learn exactly what the need is, rather than what you or others think it is;

- you honour the people concerned by listening to them, so they feel heard and valued;
- it lays the groundwork for their involvement.

Further, by communicating with them, you are not only using your strengths and assets but also using theirs. Some helpful things you can do to maximize the usefulness of the exchange include:

- undertake a needs assessment/survey;
- ask questions such as, 'What do you love about our community? What would you most like to change?'
- summarize the positive characteristics of your neighbourhood in a short phrase, such as, 'My neighbourhood is friendly and hospitable,' and start using it as much as possible;
- write an advert or create a graphic for the tourist board to attract people to your community, again flagging up the positive aspects of the area, things to do, places to go and so on;
- list the top three social issues in your community (such as loneliness, mental health difficulties, antisocial behaviour) or, if you are unsure what they are, hold a community engagement event to ask people's views;
- explore which organizations are open to partnerships (such as the police, local councils, schools).

Organizations and charities often provide useful resources to help you identify and address social needs in your community. Here are a couple of examples:

- Cinnamon Network, at: <https://cinnamonnetwork.co.uk/ctp-toolkit>;
- Redeeming Our Communities (ROC), community engagement events, at: <https://roc.uk.com/roc-conversation>.

Write a vision statement

Once you have done this and established what your vision is, it's important to write it down and then revisit it often. Don't just list your goals, though, also write up the research you've done, pray over it and offer it to God. Ask for feedback and revisit points that could be improved or refined.

Once you have the final statement ready, act boldly. Send it out as a press statement, with your signature and the signatures of those who are standing with you to action it.

Craft a personal vision statement

Putting together a vision statement for your own life helps you to recognize your personal 'yes' and what you should say 'no' to.

Some people prefer to think of this type of statement as a purpose statement. Your vision or purpose helps you to know what direction you want to take for your life, the people to be with and the jobs to apply to. It also helps to work out what it is that God is calling you to do or be a part of in your life.

Here are some examples of personal vision mission statements.

Example 1

My vision for my life is to share the gospel with teenagers.
I want to be the best representative of Jesus I can, with love and care.
I will give my time to serve young people who need a mentor.

Example 2

My vision for my life is to be a caring and loving wife/husband, mother/father and daughter/son to my family.
I want to be the best at my job as a fitness coach without giving all of myself away.
I will live my life to bring the best out of others and reflect the love of God to the world.

Identify your strengths.	Who is important in your life?
List five core values: 1 2 3 4 5	Reflect on how your skills can solve real-world issues.
Do you have a hope or dream for your life?	What injustice breaks your heart or gets under your skin?
What makes you unique?	Other thoughts about yourself.

Now answer the following questions.
My vision for my life is to . . .

I want to be the best . . .

I will . . .

Example 3

My vision for my life is to act as an instrument of positive and spiritual change in my family, at work and in my community.

I want to be the best mother/father and role model in my home.

I will use all the talents that God has given me and participate in all aspects of my life with energy, purpose and gratitude. I will use my talents in administration to ensure that my home is loving and calm, my workplace is productive and positive and my community is responsive and growing. I see problems in family life in my neighbourhood so, through this focus, I will provide a positive role model for my children and get involved with structures that build up families.

Personal vision statement tip from Cris

I was asked to write a personal vision statement for my life about 13 years ago. I found myself stuck and unsure what to write. After a number of hours, I was still looking at a blank page, so I got out my drawing pad and a pencil.

I drew a tree and asked myself what I wanted to be rooted in. I also asked myself what I wanted to make sure I fed on daily so I would grow. For the branches, I asked myself what was important to me and what fruit I wanted to see in my life. In among the branches, I wrote down activities that I was passionate about, the topics I felt God had put on my heart and mind, the people I knew were important to me and who I wanted to see thrive.

In the end, my vision wasn't a series of sentences or paragraphs but a drawing of the fruit that I wanted to see come from my life. I still regularly look at my tree to see if anything has changed or if I need to add anything. The reality is, it is a vision image that is organic and keeps changing, but it has allowed me to know what my big 'yes' is and what to say 'no' to.

Here is an inspiring story of the personal vision of Bex Wilson (<www.zarach.org.).

How God birthed a vision in my life

I'm a Deputy Head Teacher at the largest inner-city primary school in Leeds. After a decade in the job, hungry children, poor living conditions and social care referrals had sadly become the norm.

While teaching an 11-year-old boy, I noticed that he was scratching his tummy. He told me that he and his younger brother shared a cushion on the floor to sleep on. The cushion had bed bugs, which made his tummy itchy. There was no organization that could help, so I went halves with my dad and bought them beds. The poverty I saw in their home, their day-to-day battle just to survive, floored me. After originally ignoring a prompting to set up a bed poverty charity, God spoke to me through several random people and preachers. I knew it was a calling to act and use my time to set up Zarach. I was called to use my influence to ensure every child in our city had their basic needs met, so they can get a good night's sleep and an equal opportunity to get the best education possible at school. We had no experience, no funds and basically no clue. We've now, by God's grace, delivered 1,000 beds to children living without. On top of that, we've been able to provide so much more for our Zarach families, too, including other furniture donations, food parcels and housing support. Every seemingly dead end we arrived at (and there were some corkers!), we have prayed. We've prayed as a church, as a family and individually, and the answers to prayer that we have seen have been so glorious and so specific that it has felt like we've had a speed dial direct connection to God's throne room!

We give out brand new beds and bedding items with all our beds. One day, I prayed for God to provide us with 12 duvets, as we'd run out. I got back to my car and someone had left 12 single duvets in the car parking space next to mine. On the way to church, I told my husband that we were £400 short on what we needed to buy beds for that week's referrals. I started reading the incredibly sad referrals, trying to come up with a way to choose which children wouldn't get a bed. We prayed. During sung worship, I was singing at the top of my lungs, tears of desperation leaking down my cheeks, when a member of my church, who I had never spoken to, approached me and said that God had told her to bring a blank cheque for £400 to church and she thought it was for me! God is so good!

Discerning a vision if you are a church leader

In preparation for writing this book, we asked a number of church leaders to share how they discern a vision and communicate it. The ways in which each of them go about this process and communicate it are distinctly different from one another. That's because there are many ways to come to the same place of knowing your vision.

Sim Dendy, from Freedom Church in Romsey, described his process as follows:

A vision is a picture of a preferred future; an image that describes with words the tangible future to all those listening. A vision is about how it makes people feel and respond emotionally rather than a list of statistics.

I have found that the best way to clarify a vision is to write it down. Everyone has an idea of what the vision might be, but until it is written down, it is just talk. Read the words aloud. Do they grab you? Do they make you sit forward? Is it ambitious and inspiring? Don't try to tidy up the language too much or make everything start with the same letter. Perfection can often squeeze out creativity and life!

Then choose two or three trusted friends and ask them to listen as you present your vision. See if you can memorize the vision and tell it as a story: 'What would it look like if . . .' Be sure to use visually stimulating words, such as, 'Imagine the significant effect that we would have on every teenager in our neighbourhood if we made this idea a reality.' Next comes the hard part: ask for feedback.

Worth noting the story of Nehemiah 2.12 [(NLT)] here: 'I slipped out during the night, taking only a few others with me. I had not told anyone about the plans God had put in my heart for Jerusalem.' He had a vision for rebuilding the walls, but he didn't tell anyone else apart from 'only a few others'.

Great vision is owned. As the originator of the vision, you need to share ownership but you should never give it away or give it up to someone else. Listen to the feedback, take the comments on board and adapt if required, but don't end up with a committee-led statement, as it will lose all its power and become bland. Encourage the small team of people to ask questions to help you clarify the vision. Record your conversation so you can listen back to any ideas that sprang up as you shared your thoughts. It is often hard to remember what you just said when you are developing a vision, so record the conversation and you can go back through.

A helpful vision should be memorable and succinct, but not so short that it doesn't really say anything. For example:

- Microsoft's (when it began) was, 'A computer on every desk and in every home';
- Alzheimer's Association's is, 'A world without Alzheimer's disease';
- our church's vision is, 'To lead people in the pursuit of Jesus to see lives and communities transformed.'

The final and most important key thing is to communicate the vision well. This is really important. Many great visions have been lost through poor communication. Don't just slap your vision or mission statement on a wall and leave it there or put it on email footers or websites. Vision must be *cast* by the *vision holder*. You need to be in the room with people to help them feel what you feel. The vision should connect with people's hearts and emotions; that's why you cast the vision, to see who will get caught up in the net.

Andy Stanley states that you should 'keep repeating the vision until you are sick of it and then repeat it some more'. (I highly recommend his books *Visioneering* (Multnomah, 2005) and *Making Vision Stick* (Zondervan, 2007), and see also his article 'Vision leaks', Crupress, at: <www.cru.org/us/en/train-and-grow/leadership-training/leading-a-team/vision-leaks.html>.)

You cannot overshare the vision. It requires passion, energy, consistency and focus to communicate the vision well and often. Communicate to the church in waves. Sit with your senior leaders and present it to them. Then meet with the staff team, trustees, small group leaders, and then present it to the whole church.

Take time to set up each presentation well, create a comfortable room/space to meet in. Give them a hint so they come expectant. The environment where you share the vision will affect how it is received. If the room is cold or crowded or noisy, they won't engage, as they won't be able to hear or engage properly. Create space for questions. Take your time. Clarify.

Once you have communicated it in person with everyone in your church, plaster it everywhere. Office walls, screensavers, social media, website, create competitions to encourage engagement, email footers, local papers, signage around the building – annoy everyone with it and then teach and preach on it regularly. Pick one part of your vision and give it a whole

Sunday morning. Share it with your children and young people (if they don't understand it, you might need to rethink!) and ensure that all new people who join your church know the vision and can recite it.

And then repeat!

How do I move from vision to implementation?

There are more great ideas and visions on the cutting-room floor than all those that are ever realized. That is not meant to discourage, it is just the honest truth of it. The difference is that, when a vision comes from God, he will give you the stamina, courage and passion to see it through. That doesn't mean the preparation and hard work aren't required after all. In fact, it often means that there will be roadblocks that the evil one puts in your way to try to thwart it. We must also remember that sometimes, maybe often, done is better than perfect! Making a start on a vision is what sets us apart from many others.

Part 3
REBUILD

They replied, 'Let us start rebuilding.' So they began this good work.

But when Sanballat the Horonite, Tobiah the Ammonite official and Geshem the Arab heard about it, they mocked and ridiculed us. 'What is this you are doing?' they asked. 'Are you rebelling against the king?'

(Nehemiah 2.18b–19)

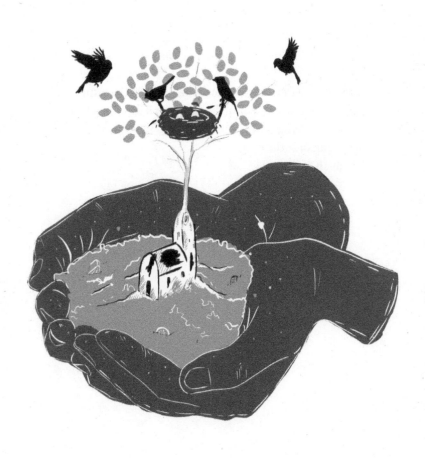

8

Reality check: future-proofing the Church

We have been on a real journey with Nehemiah already, but now we come to the fun part. We get to build and grow something that is future-minded and looks like Jesus. We are going to grow something that is future-proof!

Future-proof?

We do this by listening to God's prophetic guidance and anticipating the changes ahead that are needed to sustain life in the Church. This involves working out ways to minimize the effects of future shocks, problems or issues. It involves developing a younger leadership team and strategies for running God's mission that are robust in the face of financial stresses, then locating this mission in places where the population who need it are gathering, which may or may not be in a church. There are many other ways to future-proof the Church but these are a good start.

Because the resurrection is always pulling us forwards, we are right to ask the question, 'Does what we have at present fulfil the vision and mission that God has given us?' One thing that the COVID-19 pandemic has given us is a moment in time and particular circumstances that have allowed us to question everything. As a result, we have the opportunity to build the Church back up into something that is fit for purpose, looks more and more like Jesus and lives out his kingdom business.

As we start on this rebuilding, we must learn from the past and give ourselves the space to do things differently. What the past does not provide us with, though, is a golden moment to go back to; our culture is moving forwards, whether we like it or not. We do not and must not chase culture, however. Indeed, Jesus gives us a direct mission mandate *not* to do that very thing. Instead, we must see culture as our mission field, even allow it to help to direct the mode of the mission.

There are some glaring issues that we must also take into account. I would argue that the Church of the future must be:

- utterly dependent on Jesus;
- immersed in and attentive and obedient to the word and Spirit of God;
- more diverse;
- younger;
- smaller and more community-centred;
- led by a team, not a single, dynamic leader;
- lay leadership-focused;
- lower maintenance and have greater impact;
- focused less on gathering on Sundays and more on equipping the community of saints for action;
- emotionally open and aware;
- honest, real and authentic;
- more daring and braver;
- for those on the outside, not those on the inside.

The danger is, unless the vision, mission and direction are clear, we will build backwards, as Nehemiah did. We humans are very good at wanting what we once had and romanticizing the past. There is often a lot of pressure to build back up what is comfortable for us rather than something that is more fit for purpose.

Centres of hope

I have been much challenged by what has been happening to the Church in Iraq, reading stories from the region relayed on the Open

Doors website. In the town of Qaraqosh, Iraq, on the Nineveh Plain, there's a recently rebuilt church. When the so-called Islamic State extremists overran the region in 2014, 'cleansing' the Nineveh Plain of Christians, they set fire to the church and, later, used it as a shooting gallery. When the members of IS were ousted and some of the population returned, they rebuilt the church. Well, almost. They left a part of it in its burnt-out state, pock-marked with bullet holes. They did this so that it would serve as a reminder of their story, of those who had to flee, those who died. It is a reminder, too, to always be prepared for Christ's enemies.

This is a church that honours the ashes of loss, grief, suffering and persecution. Its people know that those ashes, ruins and rubble are nothing to be afraid of. They know that ruins are always rebuilt for one reason only: because God always keeps his promises.

It is a section of the arches that is the part which has been left unrestored. The other sections have been rebuilt, but not to the original designs. The doors now open under a banner that reads 'Centre of Hope'. The new church is a place for all the neighbourhood to come and see, taste and experience God's hope for them.

Yousif, a 21-year-old man from Qaraqosh, said to Open Doors ('Iraq: faith amid hopelessness, 9 May 2019, at: <www.opendoors. org.hk/en/28463>), 'IS can destroy our building but they can never destroy our church.' Yousif believes that even though the people in his community went through dark times, they can still smile and be happy. He went on to say:

We say to each other that we are going to rebuild this city, we are going to turn this bad situation around into a good thing. We haven't lost our faith. Me personally, I am stronger than before.

Since I came back to Qaraqosh, I've started reading my Bible again. Every night before I go to sleep, I read some verses. And when I finish reading my Bible, I talk to God. I ask him for hope, and for peace. The conversations I have with him are very special.

From the rubble, dust and dirt, the church at Qaraqosh has regrown, not as once it was but into a new centre of hope.

Leaders must relinquish power and the laity must step up

For the good of the future of the Church we, as the body of Christ, must recognize that its leadership needs to look very different from today's pattern. Gone are the days when churches could afford to have their own paid staff. We have idolized the role of church leader for far too long. In a predominantly male-led church, a culture of 'Father knows best' was created. Over time, that turned into 'the church leader knows best'. This has created an unhealthy and un-helpful culture in which the members of the congregation enjoy consuming from the learned few and the preacher enjoys being lis-tened to, deferred to and, in some extremely unhealthy cases, catered to. That is not necessarily the fault of those in leadership positions; they have simply stepped into the roles as already defined by their predecessors. The situation does, however, lend itself to harmful and unachievable standards that very few can achieve and maintain.

The present model of church leadership has created a culture in which many do not feel that they have the potential to lead, espe-cially if the current leadership does not look like them. This deskills people or, at the very least, intimates that they aren't skilled enough. This unattainable and unmaintainable culture, with a perceived holiness attached to or required of those in leadership roles, has created a cavernous gap between regular churchgoers and their church pastors, priests or ministers. It has also allowed the Church as a whole to abandon its rightful place in the holy priesthood, which Peter describes in his first letter:

You also, like living stones, are being built into a spiritual house to be a holy priesthood, offering spiritual sacrifices acceptable to God through Jesus Christ.
(1 Peter 2.5)

We are all called into this place of priesthood to live as much like Jesus as we can, carrying him into a world that needs his presence. Like the Old Testament priests, our lives must become living sacrifices to be set before the Lord each day. Our lives are now found in that of the high priest, Jesus – the body of Christ. Ordinary people have the Spirit of God anointing them for his ministry in the world. Everyone is called, needed and equipped for this task ahead. Our role and mission is to be Christ in a Christless world, to live in Christ while in the world, inviting others to live in him also and to use all resources at our disposal for his resurrection work.

Leaders, therefore, *must* release the members of the Church into this kingdom work, everyone playing their part. At the same time, the members *must* be willing to step up and to step forwards into this call.

The people need to be willing to be released

Leaders must be releasing people and the people must be willing to be released.

Whether or not you can see it, you have a call on your life to join with God in his work in the world. Whatever is in your hands can, and will, be used if you are willing. Many of us don't think that we have much to offer but, in reality, when the Spirit of God is working, your resources, character and competences – all gifts that God gave you and only you – can and should be used to build his kingdom. That starts with his Church. Don't underestimate this call or gifts by not accepting it and using them. Most importantly, don't compare your gifts to those of others as they are not called to do what you are called to do. Their story is different from yours.

What is holding you back?

As we move on to the next stage of Nehemiah's story, we will see a beautiful picture of people all playing their part in the work. Even though there was much to do and many people involved, we will also see one group of people who refused to do the work they were given. This begs the two related questions: 'Why do we not get involved?' and 'What is holding us back?'

Let us imagine the Church as a holiday cruise ship. On the ship, 80 per cent of the people are served by the remaining 20 per cent. The people of God, living out the mission of God, should be the opposite of that. We should be more like the crew on a battleship, where all are given tasks, perform them with their whole hearts and work for the greater good of the entire ship.

What holds you back from playing your part? Fear, anxiety, worry, lack of training, unsure what your part is, feeling that you are too young, too old . . . ? There are countless reasons to say 'No', to stand on the sidelines. Many of them are completely legitimate, but when God calls you to action, he is giving you a purpose to fulfil in a way that no one else can. If someone else could do it, he would call them instead. Why, then, do we say 'No' to God?

Here are some really good reasons people give.

- 'I'm emotionally exhausted right now.'
- 'I'm juggling way too many people.'
- 'I'm working every hour God sends so that I can care for my kids.'
- 'My work is really demanding at the moment.'
- 'I couldn't possibly help while I'm looking after my elderly relative.'
- 'They don't need my help, they have experts for that sort of thing.'
- 'I'd be too embarrassed.'

It could be said that these people are, in fact, serving God without even realizing it, as they are honouring others in what they are doing instead of the church projects.

Some other reasons are also totally understandable. They may not be true, but they certainly can stop us from stepping up. Sometimes we feel inferior to other gifted people and that holds us back. We might not see others like us in similar roles and that puts us off. It might be that someone hurt you or held you back before and that is stopping you this time for fear it will happen again.

However, there are some very poor reasons for not playing our part in God's work. It is easy to justify not getting involved, using reasons that look spiritual but, in fact, are not. Perhaps these sound familiar: 'I need to do more training,' 'I've got to get myself more sorted,' 'I have too much of a past.'

Whatever the reason, whether it is true or false, God is calling all of us to play our part. The individual part we are called to is appropriate to the gifts God gave us. It is also appropriate to the time and energy that we can honestly give. Don't let anyone or anything hold you back when God is asking you to step forward. Know that he has everything you need for the challenge ahead.

The Church of the future is technicolour

The Church has been monochrome for far too long. It has been monochrome in terms of its leadership and monochrome in the pews. Of course, this situation isn't simply about colour; it's also about all forms of difference and group dynamics. The Church has been led by white, educated men for centuries and the impact of this is that there has been a stagnation. Jesus' Church should look like the heavenly end time scene described in Revelation 7.9–17: a multicultural multitude 'from every nation, tribe, people and language'. This is a dynamic heavenly culture. I have used the word 'multicultural', but that is to try to describe heavenliness from our earthly perspective. It is not multicultural in that sense but God's heavenly culture at its richest, most powerful and extraordinary. It is the body of Christ looking like the fullness and glory of God. The Church of the future, therefore, should not be multicultural in the earthly sense but like the full glory of God in the heavenly sense.

God is dynamic and the Church should be too.

Knowing that and standing firm in it, we can each claim our place in this technicolour community, accepting the invitation to pick up a trowel and play our part. The people involved in this rebuilding project must be male and female, young and old, brown, black, yellow and white, recovering addicts, ex-offenders, single mums and stay-at-home dads. Those with additional needs, dyslexia, dyspraxia and those who have no clue how to change a plug. The invitation to rebuild goes out to those who can't pitch a note, have not been believers for long, been around the Church since the dawn of time and more Christian than the Archbishop of Canterbury. It goes out to those starving artists, tree huggers, latte-sippers, vegetarians and junk food eaters. It extends to those who have written themselves off, those who have spent all their money on the dogs or made their money on the stock market. It goes out further to those who are inked, pierced, have no hair, long hair, pink hair, green hair, wear a toupee, wig or weave. If you feel messed up, messed about, missing something or have a screw loose, you are invited to play your part.

Remember, a mess becomes a message with Jesus!

Don't opt out but do opt in.

That means the Church needs to be led by people who do not look like the majority. If you think you don't fit then you do fit in because the workers involved in this work all don't fit but do because of Jesus.

This has a major implication for us within the Church. We need to open the gates to those who don't look like us so they can come and play their part. We must *not* be gatekeepers but hold gates open, inviting people in. There are those God is calling who have already written themselves off because of something they think will not allow them to act on that calling. We have to open up, invite people in to play their part and give them space to be themselves in the work they do. It is *not* our job to determine their role in the kingdom; that is God's job and his alone.

The rebuilding can't be about us

If you believe that rebuilding your church or community is about getting more people in to do things, more people to sit through a sermon or more people to give financially, then give up now. Remember, the vision is Jesus, not the institution that is the Church making its way into the twenty-first century.

It will surprise no one that churches are struggling and have been for a long time. Because of this struggle, it is really easy for our activism to end up being about ourselves. The very fact that the Church is run by human beings means that it can become self-centred. We have to check on this regularly. It is not surprising that it happens when 99 per cent of those outside our church buildings aren't interested in what is happening inside them. Our true mission isn't growing the Church, it's growing the kingdom of God in every street, neighbourhood and city.

As we build our church back up, we need to consider whether it presently fulfils the mission of Jesus or is here to maintain what we already have and who we already are. This means that we need to dream bigger, be braver and boldly think outside the box. Plan for others who we do not even know yet (future-proof it). The brutal truth is that a church that loves its model more than its mission will die.

We need not to be trapped by the language of 'rebuilding' into thinking that everything can return to the way it was before the pandemic. After the Second World War, some church buildings in London were reconstructed as Christopher Wren had originally designed them. Coventry Cathedral, in contrast, was built to a completely new design by Basil Spence and made into a place that has become a peace memorial. The call that we will need to discern is whether our rebuild should be a Christopher Wren or a Basil Spence . . . and, of course, church isn't just about buildings!

In recent years, there are many who have projected that the future of the Church is online. The Church will not be permanently and solely online, however. It will need to adopt a hybrid approach, but will remain a gathering. It is the nature of family and community to gather together and the Church reflects that. While some may leave and only engage with the Church online, it does not change the fact that the Church will *always* gather because it is inherently communal.

Online churches are not the silver bullet that will change everything. They will supplement rather than replace the Church. They will serve as a shop window for people to experience something before they choose to experience it in person.

As we build the Church back up, we need to see a number of shifts take place.

- **We need to move away from being leader-focused** As mentioned previously, everyone has a part to play and should be set free to contribute in the way they were created to. We need to move away from the dynamic leader model to one of a community and family on a mission together.
- **Smaller not bigger** We should explore growing smaller, not bigger. We have idolized size for far too long. We don't need one big church serving a city but multiple Jesus communities, like a tapestry across regions. Big buildings require maintenance but meeting in living rooms, kitchens and community halls and the local parish church means that people can walk to church and meet others nearby who love Jesus.
- **We need new shapes for church communities and mission** The structures and shapes we currently have are roadblocks to where

we want to be. We need to shift towards new ways to gather and share the good news. We also need to look for new, and possibly old, ways to gather, commission and set people going on putting the mission of Jesus into effect. It is about the gathered Church working together to achieve the mission of the Church. We need to explore new options for believers to live this Jesus way of life.

- **We need to simplify** Ministries need to be simplified so that they complement people's lives rather than compete with them. Church is not the main event – life is the main event – so we need to help people to live for Jesus in their spheres rather than want them to be people running things for us. For too long the Church has been the source of ministries, but in the Gospels, it was happening in people's everyday lives. We need to be a people who are equipped to do the stuff and not asked to live out our faith in a Christian bubble.

The centrality of Scripture

We have been exploring the first half of the book of Nehemiah, but we can't miss the importance of the second half. The physical walls of the city are rebuilt and then comes the spiritual life of the city. In Nehemiah chapter 8, Ezra, the teacher of the Law, brings out the book of Moses to be read to all the people. This is a significant moment. The statement this makes is that the people of God need to come back to a place where worship, adoration and the reading and living out of Scripture are central to their identity. Without Scripture and worship, there would be little that set them apart from all the other cities around them.

If the Church and us, her people, are to be who we have been created and saved to be, then Scripture needs to be at the heart of who we are too. Without it we will never know what the vision and mission of God is – we will turn our vision and mission into something that looks and feels good to us rather than them being good to God. Sometimes God's mission and ours are very similar, but at other times they may be worlds apart.

Scripture has to be brought to the heart of each church community and to the heart of each believer. In the book of Nehemiah, there is a lovely nudge nudge, wink wink aspect to the key moment Scripture is read. We are told (in Nehemiah 8.2) that it was brought out to the people of God to be read on the 'first day' of the seventh month. The wording 'first day' is key, as this was a new moment, a reset moment, for God's people. It was to be a pivotal time when they reset themselves in line with God's word.

Do we, the Church, need a reset moment with the word of God?

Let's not romanticize the people of Nehemiah's time too much: they had a reset moment in practice, but not in their hearts. By chapter 13, we see that God's people had still missed the point, as they were trading on the Sabbath and had turned the house of God into someone's bedroom. All the more reason for Jesus to come some 500 years later.

Today, too, we must ask ourselves if we need a reset moment. Do we need to place Scripture at the heart of what we do to direct our path?

9

Nehemiah 3: all playing their part

Eliashib the high priest and his fellow priests went to work and rebuilt the Sheep Gate. They dedicated it and set its doors in place, building as far as the Tower of the Hundred, which they dedicated, and as far as the Tower of Hananel. The men of Jericho built the adjoining section, and Zakkur son of Imri built next to them.

The Fish Gate was rebuilt by the sons of Hassenaah. They laid its beams and put its doors and bolts and bars in place. Meremoth son of Uriah, the son of Hakkoz, repaired the next section. Next to him Meshullam son of Berekiah, the son of Meshezabel, made repairs, and next to him Zadok son of Baana also made repairs. The next section was repaired by the men of Tekoa, but their nobles would not put their shoulders to the work under their supervisors.

(Nehemiah 3.1–5)

Hearts have been restored to the Lord and a renewed focus for the mission has been established. All the preparation has been done and it is now time to start the massive task ahead. Bricks need to be laid (figuratively and/or physically) and the job needs to commence. Will God's people partner with him on the mission?

Many times there is a vision and a challenge, but only a few step up to the plate to play their part to make it happen. At the heart of the Scriptures is a call to partnership with God. Genesis (2.15) starts the story of God with precisely this call: 'The LORD God took the man and put him in the Garden of Eden to work it and take care of it.' Each of us is called to tend, dress and care for creation. Jesus' death didn't just save us *from* something but also *for* something: partnership with God. Partnership, partnership, partnership is at the heart of the gospel and the Scriptures.

Nehemiah brought God's people to that point where they needed to decide: were they going to spend the time, money and energy on doing the job and partnering with God? The response from the people to Nehemiah was simple: 'Let us start rebuilding.' So, they did. The project wasn't going to move forwards without spiritual attack, challenge and heartbreak, but they still stepped out in faith.

Let us start rebuilding

Like the world in Nehemiah's time, our world, too, is broken, with broken people, attitudes and systems. Many of our communities are surrounded by rubble and desperately need help to rebuild from the ruins.

The world has been shattered and communities severely affected or even lost. Frankly, COVID-19 only exacerbated an already growing problem. As the Church, we can point and shout, 'Bad world,' but our role is to take responsibility, confess our part in the problem(s), roll up our sleeves and start to rebuild our beautiful, broken world. We are the people of the resurrection. Before Jesus, the work that Nehemiah and the people were called to was a vast restoration project. They went about restoring what had been destroyed, physically and spiritually. Because we live in the world that has already been restored by Jesus, we are not involved in the kind of restoration Nehemiah describes but, rather, we are partnering him in resurrection. Resurrection sees possibility where things look to be impossible. Resurrection sees the rubble but believes in the potential offered by the kingdom. Where there is death, in resurrection there is new life. Where old projects and buildings are derelict, in resurrection we can see dreams, hopes, visions, life.

Nehemiah rebuilt a city from the ruins. We partner with Jesus, rebuilding and resurrecting a broken world.

When we refer to rebuilding in the light of Jesus' resurrection, we mean that it encourages us to use the unusable because all things are now possible. A builder might look at old bricks and say they are too damaged. Jesus looks at the bricks and sees through the damage because of his resurrection. Jesus knows about the mess, brokenness, addiction, limits in us and simply sees his Church and all the potential it holds.

Blueprints

Nehemiah's plans for building the new city were based on drawings of what the old walls looked like. Historically, we know that the people updated some of the walls, too, but many of the foundations for them were simply built using materials from the old ones. Bricks were piled on top of what had been there before. Our rebuilding is entirely different. There is no golden age that we are aiming to restore today. We are dreaming forwards because of Jesus' resurrection. This means that we don't get our blueprints for the future from the Church of the past, we don't get the plans for our communities from the past and we don't get our image of humanity from the past. We get all of that by looking forwards through the lens of the resurrection at the prophetic images and the kingdom's mysterious vision that is to be found in Scripture and, in part, come to us from the Spirit's revelations today.

Revelation gives us a glimpse into this vision:

Then I saw 'a new heaven and a new earth,' for the first heaven and the first earth had passed away, and there was no longer any sea. I saw the Holy City, the new Jerusalem, coming down out of heaven from God, prepared as a bride beautifully dressed for her husband. And I heard a loud voice from the throne saying,

'Look! God's dwelling-place is now among the people, and he will dwell with them. They will be his people, and God himself will be with them and be their God. "He will wipe every tear from their eyes. There will be no more death" or mourning or crying or pain, for the old order of things has passed away.'
(Revelation 21.1–4)

The call to the hands and hearts of the Church is to be a part of this resurrection vision. It is the new Jerusalem city life, where God is present with his people and tears, death, hopelessness, pain, suffering, hunger, disease are gone. This is the blueprint for our communities too.

Many of us struggle to understand the end times, so may have absorbed the wrong theology on this topic. We often think that it's about a mass evacuation to a better place, but the book of Revelation paints this incredible picture of heaven and earth coming together. In its words we can see that this place, our home, will be restored, resurrected and reclaimed so it can become what it was always intended to be.

This blueprint for what will happen was first witnessed and spoken about in Isaiah 61. Jesus read from this passage in the synagogue in Nazareth:

The Spirit of the Sovereign LORD is on me,
    because the LORD has anointed me
    to proclaim good news to the poor.
He has sent me to bind up the broken-hearted,
    to proclaim freedom for the captives
    and release from darkness for the prisoners,
to proclaim the year of the LORD's favour
    and the day of vengeance of our God,
to *comfort all who mourn*,
    and *provide for those who grieve* in Zion –

to *bestow on them a crown of beauty*
   instead of ashes,
the *oil of joy*
   instead of mourning,
and a *garment of praise*
   instead of a spirit of despair.
They will be called oaks of righteousness,
   a planting of the LORD
   for the display of his splendour.
(Isaiah 61.1–3, italics added)

This passage is a messianic text. Yes, it's about Jesus but it's also about God's people living out what the Messiah started. This coming together of heaven and earth in the lives of God's people is described as being something that we will witness in our earthly reality at some point in the future. We also have the benefit of the 'helper' – the same Holy Spirit that raised Christ from the grave is described here as coming for the anointing of God's people. This life, lived with the Spirit, is for our commissioning and empowering today, too, so that we might see the world around us shaped more like the heavenly reality. It's about us as God's people seeing this 'God reality' creep into our lives today.

A future reality can be seen today because of the work of the Spirit, because the kingdom of King Jesus is here, there and near. The kingdom can be seen now by Christians, growing through the cracks in the pavements like wildflowers. The kingdom of heaven trickles through all the broken and damaged parts of the world.

Nehemiah's plans were about physical walls, gates, doors, passageways. The blueprints for the Church today are about bricks, mortar, blood, sweat and tears, families, communities, real lives, real people, dust and dirt, grass and street corners. They are both about having radically different, Holy Spirit-inspired visions that lead to new heavens, new communities and new lives.

The people of Nehemiah's day said, 'Let us start rebuilding'; do we, as the Church, do the same today? Do we boldly step into our part in this resurrection project? Do you? Are you willing to dedicate your hands to this work?

The technicolour community

Chapter 3 in the book of Nehemiah records the big moment for the work of rebuilding. We can see two very distinct groups of people through some interesting revelations of their characters. First, we see those who committed to the vision and got stuck in. Woven into the tapestry of chapter 3 are the names of those who got involved and got their hands dirty.

The chapter begins with Eliashib, the high priest, and his fellow priests. The priests led the way. It was their initial hard work that saw the Sheep Gate being rebuilt. The significance of this is not to be overlooked. The role of the priest was (and still is today) to lead the way and to open it up so others can then follow. The priests didn't sit back and wait for others to start first; they didn't think that they were above doing the work. They got into the nitty-gritty as the beautiful servants priests should be. What is revealed to us here foreshadows the supreme High Priest who would wash feet, feed the hungry and, ultimately, give his own life on the cross for his people.

The opening line of chapter 3 therefore points us to the importance of good leadership. Good leaders get involved in whatever task is in hand. They play their part by showing their commitment to the work, by physically taking part and, often, kicking things off. Nehemiah's priests couldn't do all the work themselves, though, and it is right that they weren't expected to. The role of the priest is to lead by example, setting others up to get involved. The priests thus started the work and then we read that others took up their sections and worked on them in their way.

We also learn that others were involved: merchants, perfume makers, goldsmiths, stonemasons, rulers, roofers, temple servants, city security guards, residents from Jericho, residents from the local area, families from all over. In the list of workers, we also find artists, builders and cloth sellers. It's a total mishmash, a motley crew. Everyone was invested in the project, everyone mucked in. We see that administrators helped to organize the work and security guards left their posts to do some pointing of the brickwork. People played out of their usual positions to do what was needed.

Nehemiah names families and tribes from all around Jerusalem. People from Hazor, Bethel, Jericho, Bethlehem, Tekoa, Beth-zur, Keilah, Abuliam, Zorah, Gezer, Mizpeh, Gibeon. People with different skills from different locations came together as one people. This conjures up an image something like an episode of *DIY SOS*. It was an all-hands-on-deck project where every empty hand was encouraged to grab a trowel, a bucket of cement or simply a brush to sweep up the debris.

The image also suggests that anyone who wanted to get involved was welcomed. However, a second group of people is revealed to us who were not so willing to help:

> The next section was repaired by the men of Tekoa, but their nobles would not put their shoulders to the work under their supervisors.
> (Nehemiah 3.5)

Within the image that Nehemiah paints for us, we understand that each tribe was tasked with a different section of the city. Some were on wall duty while others set about repairing gates, roads and so on. One particular section of the wall was headed up by the men of Tekoa. In fact, Tekoa, still there today, is an Israeli settlement, organized, at the time of writing, as a community on the West Bank, about 16 kilometres south of Jerusalem. Back then, the men of Tekoa came to help with the rebuilding but the noblemen declined to do the hard work as they believed that they were above this sort of thing.

Woven throughout Nehemiah 3 are examples and the names of people who had vast political and social influence. The chapter is full of mentions of gifted people for whom labouring on a building site would not have been part of their usual working day. They would normally have been found in the equivalent of office jobs and the law courts, not on building sites, but they were there, willing to do their bit. They joined the team, got stuck in and did what had to be done. That is why the comment in verse 5 about the nobles from Tekoa stands out as a jarring note, like an awkward silence. Who did they think they were?

It is curious that they refused to get involved. In truth, however, the nature of the work was all about people being willing to help – no one was forced. The vision was set and people were asked to make it happen, but they didn't have to.

Perhaps Nehemiah included this information to serve as a reminder that there will always be those who decide not to join in. Indeed, we have all been part of events or gatherings where there are some who are happier chatting in the corner than getting on with the practical things that need to be done.

Perhaps, too, he included it to serve as a challenge to us to reflect on how we handle such situations.

- Are there roles that we think are beneath us?
- Are there roles that we think others should do?
- Have you ever found yourself saying, 'I'm happy to help but I'm not going to do that job'?

For some, helping can be more of a social activity than involving doing any or much of the hard graft themselves. The nobles, similarly, may have wanted the glory of being associated with the work without getting their own hands dirty. Do we do the same? It is worth asking ourselves about the truth of this in relation to our own approach to and participation in projects. There is a danger that we sometimes pick and choose the work we get involved in. Worse still is the spiritual excuse given: 'That is not my gift.' True, there are times when this is very appropriate but, be honest, are there other times when you are called to work and find an excuse not to do it?

The blueprint for how to how to handle this and any other such situation is the actions of Jesus, the Servant King. Jesus is the noble one who is also willing to put his back into the work. Just take a look at Jesus' curriculum vitae. For most of his young life, Jesus worked as what in the Greek is a *tekton*. Though often thought of as a carpenter, *tekton* is better translated as 'craftsman'. The term is frequently contrasted in the region of Nazareth with those of 'blacksmith' and 'stone-worker' or 'mason'. In a nutshell, Jesus worked in hard conditions and would have had the hands of a workman.

Then there is the moving example he set us when he took off his outer garments, right down to his underwear, and washed his disciples' feet as a way of apprenticing them in having the heart of a servant. Jesus shows us his heart as our Servant King. There is no job that is beneath him. There is nothing that he is unwilling to do for the kingdom:

Who, being in very nature God,
　　did not consider equality with God something to be used to
　his own advantage;
rather, he made himself nothing
　　by taking the very nature of a servant,
　　being made in human likeness.
And being found in appearance as a man,
　he humbled himself
　　by becoming obedient to death –
　　　even death on a cross!
(Philippians 2.6–8)

The differences between this and the actions of the nobles of Tekoa are obvious. The nobles were not willing to lower themselves to do physical labour, even break a sweat, while Jesus, who is of the highest nobility, always jumped in because of his servant heart.

Leaders who get their hands dirty

Most of us aren't called to be leaders in the traditional sense, but we are all people with influence. We are called to use that influence to point people to Jesus and do what we can to see God's mission accomplished. Sadly, sometimes leaders can become filled with their own self-importance and leave the rubbish jobs for those they see as beneath them. Nehemiah offers encouragement to all of us not to do that. The gates in the city wall were each for specific tasks and roles. Some of the gates were prestigious and used for specific festivals; others were there for much humbler day-to-day tasks:

The Dung Gate was repaired by Malkijah son of Rekab, ruler of the district of Beth Hakkerem. He rebuilt it and put its doors with their bolts and bars in place.
(Nehemiah 3.14)

The Dung Gate was where all of Jerusalem's unclean waste and rubbish was put before being taken down to the Valley of Hinnom, where it would be burned. It was the exit for the dead animals, rotting food, all manner of vile things. Its name says it all. Malkijah was a nobleman and his job was to rebuild the toilet gate.

His actions are a perfect contrast to those of the noblemen of Tekoa. Malkijah, in all likelihood, would have preferred a different task, but he understood its necessity, was committed to the vision and got busy rebuilding. All leaders need to take note of Malkijah's attitude and get involved in serving, taking the hardest stuff on, not just the sexy or easy jobs.

The place of worship in the rebuild

The task of the rebuilding isn't separate from the need to worship. Serving, working and building go hand in hand with worship. It is important to see every moment as a moment to worship.

> Therefore, I urge you, brothers and sisters, in view of God's mercy, to offer your bodies as a living sacrifice, holy and pleasing to God – this is your true and proper worship.
> (Romans 12.1)

This sentiment is echoed throughout Scripture, and one example is in Nehemiah:

> Eliashib the high priest and his fellow priests went to work and rebuilt the Sheep Gate. They dedicated it and set its doors in place.
> (Nehemiah 3.1a)

They dedicated the gate as soon as it was built. This was the first gate to be completed but, before they went any further, they dedicated it to God as an act of worship. Their hard work was pointed directly and intentionally at God, and it was to be seen as sacred and holy.

There is always the danger that, in our hearts, when we do this, we worship the work, the task or the plans rather than God, who cast the vision in the first place. The priests led the people in their rebuilding of the city but then made sure that the work was dedicated to God. It was a consequential and significant moment. It meant that they were then also worshipping as the wall grew around the city. They didn't wait until the end to worship, but worshipped throughout the entire process, celebrating each small breakthrough, each gate, each brick that was placed.

The priests at the first gate celebrated what God had done in building the one gate. They wanted to make sure that the glory went to the right place, not to themselves. They gave thanks for each small moment and worshipped God for what he had done and what he was doing, not the final outcome. This kept the vision at the forefront of their minds. It also helped to reinforce the role that they played in its fruition.

Lessons from Nehemiah 3

Everyone had a role in the reconstruction of the city and the realization of the vision, every community had its own area of responsibility and section to complete, and this made a mission that brought together everyone in a way that they had not experienced in generations. The vision and mission unified the people around the common task.

This was a team effort that required complete commitment from everyone. As we read through the list of workers, we recognize just what a team effort it was, the walls and gates being rebuilt sometimes by professional, skilled workers and other times by amateurs. Ideally, this is the way the Church should always operate. Church leaders are not meant to be one-person bands who each do everything in their church while the other members sit on their seats, waiting to be served. Neither should they be dictators, doling out tasks that they feel are beneath them. We all have different gifts, but they are to be used to edify and build up all. As Paul writes:

> So Christ himself gave the apostles, the prophets, the evangelists, the pastors and teachers, to equip his people for works of service, so that the body of Christ may be built up until we all reach unity in the faith and in the knowledge of the Son of God and become mature, attaining to the whole measure of the fullness of Christ.
> (Ephesians 4.11–13)

You will notice from this that the gifts given to leaders enable them to equip the people of God for mission. Evangelists weren't given so the Christians could hear the message but that the non-believers would hear it. These gifts, then, are so the whole Church will be built up but also so the world will hear and receive the good news. This is what we learn from Nehemiah too. Some may have been gifted in particular areas, and they were to work in those areas, but all also helped in whatever ways they could.

With this in mind, we must ask ourselves:

- 'Am I willing to join in and play my part?'
- 'Am I willing to do things that I am not skilled at, because the mission is bigger than me?'
- 'Am I willing to do things that make me a servant and not a leader?'
- 'Am I willing to put the work in, not stand back and watch others take everything on?'

Also, although our skills may not look like an obvious fit for the task given to us, we never know how we might be used, as Nehemiah's team found.

> Uzziel son of Harhaiah, one of the goldsmiths, repaired the next section; and Hananiah, one of the perfume-makers, made repairs next to that. They restored Jerusalem as far as the Broad Wall.
> (Nehemiah 3.8)

The important thing to remember is that though you may not know how you fit or what God's call on your life is, don't think you have nothing to offer. If a goldsmith and a perfume maker can roll up their sleeves and repair a wall, then surely each one of us can help in some way to build up the Church!

10

Yes, but how?

With Debra Green and Paul Weston

Under Nehemiah's leadership, the walls of the city were rebuilt. As we have seen, he inspired others to work alongside him and take ownership with him of the vision to achieve this. The work was challenging and they faced opposition along the way, but the wall was completed in 52 days.

As Christians, we are called, like Nehemiah, to be servants for the kingdom. That might mean rebuilding a wall, restoring relationships, renewing our communities – all forms of reversing the destruction brought about by the evil one. In being his servants, we partner with Jesus to rebuild and resurrect parts of our broken world.

What does this rebuilding look like for us? Every church addresses different needs, as we have different challenges in our local communities, ranging from poverty to mental health issues, knife crime to gaps in health care provision, homelessness to the environment, to name a few. The needs are great and those willing to do the work are exhausted.

Where does our help come from? The words Jesus quoted from Isaiah in the previous chapter bear repetition here:

> The Spirit of the Sovereign LORD is on me,
>   because the LORD has anointed me
>   to proclaim good news to the poor.
> He has sent me to bind up the broken-hearted,
>   to proclaim freedom for the captives
>   and release from darkness for the prisoners,

to proclaim the year of the LORD's favour
    and the day of vengeance of our God,
to comfort all who mourn,
    and provide for those who grieve in Zion –
to bestow on them a crown of beauty
    instead of ashes,
the oil of joy
    instead of mourning,
and a garment of praise
    instead of a spirit of despair.
(Isaiah 61.1–3)

Teamwork

Nehemiah painted a picture of a diverse group of people who were involved in the rebuilding, from rulers to roofers. Some were tradespeople and others simply listed as being residents. Families from all over were involved, including small children.

The emphasis in Nehemiah chapter 3 is not on being highly skilled in order to take part but, rather, on a willingness to be involved. God does use our skills and experience, but our availability is the most important thing. As Dr Sunday Adelaja says, 'To be able to impact society and to be an agent of change, you have to make yourself available to serve' (<www.quoteslyfe.com/quote/To-be-able-to-impact-the-society-30892>).

Remember how the nobles of Tekoa came but refused to work (Nehemiah 3.5)? How they felt that they were above doing the lowest job? Our attitude to service is a big deal. God wants open hearts and willing hands.

Who might share your vision and work with you?

Find a few people who share a similar concern and might be willing to join in to tackle it. Here are some teamwork tips that you may find helpful.

- Make teamwork a priority and reward instances of it.
- Clarify roles, responsibilities and accountabilities.
- Set clear goals.
- Communicate with one other.
- Make decisions together.
- Build trust and get to know one another better.
- Celebrate differences/diversity.

How to rebuild our communities

What is inspirational about the book of Nehemiah is that all the different tribes and communities come together to rebuild the walls and gates of the city. How can we take that inspiration and apply it to our situations today? What are we called to rebuild? Perhaps it is the Church, perhaps it is the vision of the Church or maybe, just maybe, it is to build our churches away from the traditional buildings, taking the Church out to the people instead of expecting the people to come to us. How can we live out the message of the Church in the streets and neighbourhoods near us? How can they be built, practically, as a sign of compassion?

Church involvement in social action has increased exponentially in the past 20 years. The update to the National Churches Trust 2020 report, 'The house of good', reported that the research showed the total economic and social value of the 40,300 churches to the UK was £12.4 billion (at: <www.houseofgood.nationalchurchestrust.org>).

Below are some ideas for groups, activities and events that will enable your church to engage with the local community, plus some others to get the ball rolling as you work to identify and grow relevant social action projects:

- run an afternoon play scheme;
- hold dance or DJ workshops;
- arrange a local community party, with games for kids and their parents;
- create a mural that depicts community values;
- clean local shop windows and touch up paintwork;
- hold multi-sports tournaments;
- set up craft/painting activities;
- organize a litter pick;
- decorate the community centre;
- have a water fight (invite the fire brigade!);
- ask your local hospice how you can bless them;
- arrange a gardening project and hedge cutting;
- repair damage caused by vandalism or remove graffiti;
- help elderly local people in practical ways;

- create a bicycle and skateboard hospital;
- construct a new play facility;
- organize an animal hospital session (invite the RSPCA);
- create a health awareness campaign with the local surgery;
- wrap up your week with a free BBQ;
- plant a fruit tree or even an orchard;
- plan a social action project for your community based on an unmet need;
- work together with other churches and organizations to lend support or find solutions to a local issue;
- send a letter of thanks to an MP, teacher, police officer or someone else who is working hard to serve your community.

Here are stories of tangible outcomes that resulted from acting on the kinds of ideas that are listed above. The first is a project I was involved in.

> Following a community engagement event we conducted in Preston, litter was listed as one of the top issues. A group of five agencies, including a church, housing association, primary school, local council and the local chip shop, worked together on a community litter pick. We produced a flyer with all five logos. There was such a sense of teamwork and community spirit.

Seeing the poverty and need in the neighbourhood at the time of the pandemic, Paul Weston, leader of New Generation Church, based in south east London, and members of the church responded in a variety of ways through the Blackfen Community Library and a community charity, Lark in the Park. Paul writes:

> Church members volunteered to deliver medicines from the local pharmacy, helped with deliveries and stock rotation at

the Bexley Foodbank, and cooked meals and shopped for their vulnerable neighbours. We started a free school in 2013 called Hope Community School. Our school chaplain works hard serving the families of Hope Community School. Our chaplain also has text-messaging groups for giving support.

Every Christmas, we give away hampers to our community, for local heroes or those who had a tough time, and 2020 was no exception. We gave away 45 luxury hampers and raised around £1,600, with £400 given as gifts to two of those nominated. Through this difficult time our church also set up a hardship fund, which has so far given away £3,000 and helped countless people – those needing to fix/repair appliances, help with the gap before getting universal credit, supported an injured, self-employed person and many more.

Throughout the year we give chocolates to our local police team to thank them for their hard work and service, deliver gifts to all our church members who are teachers and all the staff at Hope Community School for 'Thank a teacher' day. As a church we have maintained connection with our members through regular phone calls. We make a point of offering emotional and practical help. It is hard for some to ask for help but when it is offered, we find it is easier for them to say 'Yes'. Video calls for small group meetings and online church services were quickly set up to stay connected. We recently started the Hot Food Project at our community centre, as part of the local authority outreach to the community. This is currently providing a weekly hot meal for five local families. Additionally, Lark in the Park, our community charity, created an online event during the summer and some COVID-secure in-person kids' puppet shows. We had more than 2,000 views on YouTube for our online content. We also cleared gardens and litter-picked the local area.

Blackfen Community Library and Rooted Coffee House

have gone above and beyond in providing the following during the last year:

- free lunches for children;
- book deliveries, prescription pick-up and shopping;
- weekly video calls with volunteers;
- kids' puppet shows via video call;
- online quiz nights;
- 250 kids' craft bags given away;
- kids' Christmas window art display with prizes;
- kids' treasure hunt in shop windows;
- activities for kids during the Christmas holidays;
- digital devices sourced and provided for those in need.

To learn more about what New Generation is doing and for some other ideas, check out their websites at:

- <www.newgen.org.uk>
- <www.newgen.org.uk/lark-in-the-park>
- <https://blackfencommunitylibrary.org>
- <www.hopecommunityschool.org>

Now, Rachel Jordan-Wolf, of HOPE Together, shares some tips on how to rebuild in unity.

On the night before Jesus died on the cross, he prayed, and he included you and me in his prayers. What did he pray for? He prayed that we would be one – united.

Being one was so important to Jesus as it models the unity of the Trinity, demonstrates God's glory and speaks eloquently to the world of his love for us, which is reflected in our love for one another. As we think about rebuilding post the pandemic, there has to be a deep desire to do so as one people, because Jesus has this deep desire for us.

I work for HOPE Together and we recognize that unity matters. We began in 2008 by drawing churches, denominations and agencies together for an intentional year of mission and evangelism. A report commissioned on HOPE 08 noted how much local churches had worked together in unity during the year; many of those united groups are still working together. HOPE Together has unity in mission in its DNA and works with a wide range of partners, different denominations and mission agencies with the sole aim that 'everyone everywhere knows Jesus'. As we pull out of the COVID years, let's do this together, coalescing around mission and evangelism.

How can we work together?
How can we work together when there is so much we don't agree on? A simple agreement on the gospel is sufficient for unity in mission, such as, 'Christ died for our sins according to the Scriptures, that he was buried, that he was raised on the third day.' If we can agree on this, we have a basis for unity in mission.

Praying together
We start by praying together that all might have the opportunity to know Jesus. Praying together releases common vision and builds genuine relationships.

Be genuine
How do we go deeper? Unity needs genuine relationships that develop over time. Praying side by side and actively serving side by side creates relationships that last. Getting to know one another over food can be really powerful.

Cultural divides
What about cultural and ethnic church divides? HOPE has worked to build partnerships with those in ethnically diverse

church denominations, listening first, attending the others' events before expecting people to come to us, sacrificing our preferences and listening; that's where we start.

Let's keep unity and working with the whole family a meaningful part of how we rebuild. We are not one family on mission together if we don't rebuild by working and praying together.

Diversity

On 25 May 2020, a 46-year-old African American named George Floyd died in police custody after a white police officer knelt on his neck for a period of 8 minutes and 46 seconds during his arrest. The incident was filmed by an onlooker and the footage showing the police officer's persistence, Mr Floyd pleading for his life, went viral around the globe.

George Floyd's death triggered massive protests across the USA and in other parts of the world, including the UK. An outpouring of centuries of pain and frustration saw a groundswell of protest against racism in the USA and globally, and a campaign using the hashtag #BlackLivesMatter on social media. What followed was a call for all organizations, businesses and charities – including churches – to take a long, hard look at their complicity in a systemic issue that has been around for generations. Many are making efforts to address the systematic racism prevalent in our culture and in our communities, some are simply making gestures and some are doing very little. Here is what you can do to tackle this issue head on.

- **Ask your church about its policy on tackling racism** How diverse is the leadership, staff and speaker team and what plans are in place to address any lack of diversity? Does the level of diversity in your church reflect that of the wider community? Encourage your church to partner with minority ethnic groups to inform your church's response to the #BlackLivesMatter movement and issues of racism. If you are a white majority or white-led church, ask how you can engage more effectively with and learn from the response of black-led denominations.

- **Ask your church to pray publicly about racism** Ask your church leader to create space to publicly and regularly pray against issues of racism in corporate settings, for the UK context and globally.
- **Ask your church about anti-racist teaching and education** Do your church leaders and members of staff offer any anti-racism education or training? Is your church actively seeking to lead the congregation in this area? If not, suggest how the church might do (such as via a book club, in sermons or seminars).
- **Ask how your church can support its black, Asian and minority ethnic neighbours** Could your church financially support grass-roots organizations that serve your community? How could your church best champion and support the work of black majority churches in your area? Are there local anti-racism organizations and initiatives in your community that your church could partner with?
- **Ask your church how its members are proactively addressing diversity in the church** Not only does your church need to fight for equality and social justice in the context of racism but it also needs to address diversity across a number of other areas. Talk to your church leadership team about how you might challenge proactively unjust structures, systems and power dynamics, in both your own community and nationally.

Additional needs, disability and accessibility

The Church hasn't always borne in mind those who have additional needs when planning how it will function. The body of Christ is made up of people from all tribes, nations and tongues, those with learning needs, disabilities visible and invisible and chronic illness. Each and every one of us is welcomed into the family as children of God, so we all need to be able to access its worship and community life.

The pandemic made us reconsider what and where the Church is, and how we can be a church family together, alongside those who have, in the past, been unable to access our buildings and our worship.

The key word here is 'together'. We have to ask ourselves the question, 'Can everyone within our church family, at home or in the building, access the life of the church and the way we worship in full?'

If not, how do we rebuild the church for everyone, not just the majority?

Come alongside

It is important that we travel this road with all who belong to our church families, including those with disabilities, additional needs and chronic illness. The aim should be not to consider how we do things to and for them but, rather, to ensure that we travel alongside them. We should find ways to involve those who cannot be physically present as well as those who can, including them in decisions and fully enveloping them in the life of their local church.

The Church moving online during the pandemic made it possible for those previously unable to use their gifts to once again preach, lead parts of worship and more, and we are the richer for it.

We have family at home

We should not and must not move back to people not being able to access church. Any rebuilding and renewal must acknowledge that the Church encompasses the homes of those who cannot leave them. It also gives us opportunities to see how we can facilitate coming into the church building for anyone who wants to and has struggled to do so in the past.

Dignity, respect and love

There is no magic formula for including disabled people in the rebuilding of our churches. It's actually quite simple. If we view those with disabilities, additional needs and chronic illness like any other part of our family and treat them with dignity, respect and love, that will take us a long way along the road towards being inclusive. There will be things that need to be done to support access, but sitting down and talking with people and then understanding those things we can do to make taking part less of a struggle are vital. The changes needed will often help lots of other people too.

We may need to be brave with our technology, beaming contributions into the building as well as live streaming out. We also need to be creative in how we take the church to people. Church can be sitting in the park with a family whose children cannot access Sunday worship owing to additional needs. It can be taking coffee and cake to share with someone who cannot leave the house.

Getting help

As we plan for the Church to really serve and be accessible to everyone, we might need some help. Many of us aren't aware of the struggles people go through with our churches. Unless those affected are very vocal, we may miss the small and easy changes that can make the world of difference. We must ask those who can give us the information we need.

If you would like some support in this area, we can highly recommend, for children and families, the Additional Needs Alliance (at: <https://additionalneedsalliance.org.uk>). For general church support and advice, Through the Roof is very helpful (at: <www.throughtheroof.org/forchurches>).

Creation care

In 2015, the historic Paris agreement was adopted at the UN climate talks. There, 196 countries agreed to cut their carbon emissions and phase out the use of highly polluting fossil fuels in order to keep the global rise in temperature to well below 2 °C, to slow down the catastrophic effects of global warming on the Earth and its inhabitants.

The follow-up set of key talks were held in Glasgow in 2021, and it is not overstating the gravity of the situation to say that the fate of the world rests on how well what has been agreed is implemented and what the various nations around the world do next.

What, then, as Christians, should we make of the future prospects for the world? Does our faith shape our perspective on these issues? Do we, in fact, have something unique to offer the world at this time of crisis, as we consider how to play our part in saving the world, knowing the one who is saviour?

Environmentalist and theologian Dr Ruth Valerio, Director of Global Advocacy at Tearfund, offers six ways in which we can all be involved in creation care.

- **Pray** As Christians, our first call when we see the world in trouble must be to turn to prayer. There is a strong biblical tradition of lament, where we cry out to God for the things that are not as they should be. There is huge significance in mourning the brokenness of the world and our interactions with it, for acknowledging the situation and recognizing our role in contributing to it, even when it has been unconscious or unintentional. From this place we can repent and look to move forwards on a new path, praying for the change we want to see in our own lives and the wider world. I strongly believe in the power of God to change situations, so let us stand together to pray for the climate and those most affected by the crisis we're in.
- **Learn** We live in a complicated world with complicated problems, where we are increasingly connected to and reliant on people on the other side of the world. My actions have effects for people I have never met. Part of our responsibility before God as Christians is learning about what's going on in his world, so that the choices we make and the actions we take are conscious and well informed. I talk lots more about these

issues in my books, *Just Living* (Hodder & Stoughton, 2017), *L Is for Lifestyle* (IVP, 2019) and *Saying Yes to Life* (SPCK, 2019), and on my blog, so do use these to explore and find out more. Tearfund has, for many years, been campaigning and taking action to address the climate crisis and help those in poverty who are most affected and you can learn more and get involved with our work by signing up to our Tearfund Action emails.

- **Speak up**   We are also called, as Christians, to stand up for justice, asking those in positions of power to make decisions that protect the most vulnerable people and the Earth we all rely on. One hugely important issue that we must hold governments to account for is slashing carbon emissions, which are the cause of global heating and a massive contributor to the climate crisis we are experiencing. Alongside meeting the requirements of the Paris agreement, in the UK, this means delivering net zero carbon emissions as quickly as possible. Additionally, we must call for alignment of our national contribution to keep us on track for 1.5 °C of heating globally, as well as using our diplomatic influence to press other countries to do the same. We need to demand that all overseas investments are compatible with the aims of the Paris agreement, moving away entirely from fossil fuels, and increasing investment in zero-carbon energy development. One way to join with others in lobbying the government in the UK is through The Climate Coalition, a network of more than 100 organizations, made up of 19 million individuals, all dedicated to action against global heating.

Another important issue that we need to see governments tackle is rubbish, particularly plastic waste, which is polluting our oceans, poisoning wildlife on a huge scale and causing disease and death in many poor communities that lack appropriate waste management systems. To this end, Tearfund is running its Rubbish Campaign, so get involved! If you live outside the

UK, check out the global Renew Our World campaign, with different national campaigns being run in 13 countries, all aiming to see action on climate breakdown and waste.

- **Live**   As well as asking others to act, we must look at our own lives and lifestyles, considering where we might need to make changes to be kinder to the planet and the people we share it with, taking responsibility for our part in creating the crisis we are now in through our own consumer habits and high resource use. Being part of the problem means that we can also be part of the solution!

  There are lots of steps we can take in our ordinary lives to make changes and help resolve these issues. We must all change our eating habits to a predominantly vegetable and grain-based diet, buying local and seasonal produce and prioritizing organic products wherever possible. We must use less-polluting means of travel to get around, such as public transport, car shares or electric cars – and, of course, flying significantly less, or not flying at all, is one of the most effective things we can do. We can switch our domestic energy supplier to one that uses 100 per cent renewable energy or even have solar panels installed, as well as planting trees and reducing our energy use when we can (such as by choosing energy-efficient appliances and turning things off wherever possible). We can reduce our waste, particularly plastic (which never fully breaks down and so is around for ever). This is a journey I have been on for the past few years, alongside others, on my Plastic-Less Living Facebook group, so do join me there! Alongside reducing, reusing and recycling are important, with the ultimate aim being the bare minimum going to landfill. For more ideas and tips, visit the Green Living pages on my website <ruthvalerio.net/green-living/>.

- **Give**   The way we choose to spend our money shows us what we value. As Jesus says in Luke 12.34, 'Where your treasure is, there your heart will be also.' We can talk about these issues all we like but unless we are using our own resources to make a difference, it is all in vain. And it is not just the money we give away that we need to consider, but also the money we keep and spend. With the money that we keep, we should think about our bank accounts, investments and pensions – are the places where we are storing our money (and earning interest) doing so in an ethical way that does not harm other people and the Earth? And how about the money we spend and the things we buy – are we considering how to be ethical consumers, making decisions that respect our global neighbours and the natural world?

For the money we give away, are we doing so generously? Our giving should reflect God's care for the whole of his creation – people and the rest of the natural world – so donating to organizations that are addressing both is the best way forward. One of Tearfund's corporate priorities is environmental and economic sustainability, which sees it empowering those living in poverty in ways that also allow the natural world to flourish, for example through programmes using climate-smart agriculture and off-grid renewable energy. A Rocha is another Christian organization that works to engage communities in nature conservation to protect God's beautiful creation. Christian Aid is also campaigning to see a move from fossil fuels, which are causing climate change, to renewable energy, to build a cleaner, safer world for all, particularly those living in poverty. And there are many other wonderful organizations that are dedicated to this dual purpose of protecting people and the planet, so get stuck in and support them!

- **Share** Alongside our own personal actions, we need to share and join with other Christians in our churches to respond together. And there are many churches across the world that are doing just that! After many years, the sleeping giant that is the Church is starting to wake up, making a huge difference in communities in many countries: from Huay Mai Duei Church in Thailand getting involved in waste collection in its area where rubbish is a big problem, to Trinity Christian Reformed Church in Michigan, USA, promoting creation care in its preaching and adopting a nearby stretch of creek to look after, to the Church of God in Mendoza, Argentina, starting a litter-picking scheme in the central park, for which it has won an award! And there is the potential to make an even greater impact, with around a third of the world's population adhering to the Christian faith, making it the biggest group of people on the planet.

In our own churches we can take inspiration from those who have naturally incorporated caring for creation into sermons and prayers in their services, who have done community litter picks and started to use recycled materials for their toddler groups that would otherwise have been binned. Some have committed to selling Fairtrade products in their cafés and collecting food waste or putting on plant-based community lunches. Others are switching to renewable energy or installing their own solar panels. Some are involved with toilet twinning, tree planting or the climate strikes, and others are replacing disposable cups and cutlery with reusable ones. The list could go on! There are so many ways, big and small, that our churches can start to have an impact straight away, joining with brothers and sisters around the world, to care for God's creation. A Rocha UK's Eco Church scheme is a great way to see where your church is on the journey and give you ideas on how you could do more. To get inspired, why not visit its stories page (<ecochurch.arocha.org.uk/stories/>) to see what other churches have been doing?

Note that many of the ideas featured in the above list are taken from my books, so do see *Saying Yes to Life*, *L Is for Lifestyle* and *Just Living*, mentioned above, for a more in-depth exploration of these issues, plus *Planet Protectors* (SPCK, 2021), which I wrote with Paul Kerensa for children.

Also, check out the Intergovernmental Panel on Climate Change report (at: <www.ipcc.ch>).

The persecuted Church

Seeing the needs of the global Church and playing our part in responding is key to the restoration of the world. Here are some practical ways in which we can celebrate with, learn from and serve our brothers and sisters who are being persecuted. With thanks to Emma Worrell of Open Doors for the following ideas.

- We all love receiving a letter or a card in the post. Send hope to Christians living in the context of persecution – let them know that they're not forgotten (see how at: <www.opendoorsuk.org/act/letter>).
- Worship with secret Christians. Step into their shoes and pray with them as they risk it all for Jesus. Run Secret Church at your church (see: <www.opendoorsuk.org/secretchurch>).
- Learn the faith lessons of the early Church and those closest to them, the contemporary persecuted church. Journey through the book of Acts and discover Dangerous Faith (see: <www.open doorsuk.org/dangerousfaith>).
- When life caves in, what do you do? Explore the theme of lament and loss with persecuted Christians and find God in the ashes (at: <www.opendoorsuk.org/churches/resources/among-the-ashes>).
- Respond on your feet and with action. Take part in a fundraising challenge to help rebuild communities facing persecution (at: <www.opendoorsuk.org/act/fundraise>).
- Speak up and use your voice in your spheres of influence (see: <opendoorsuk.org/act/volunteer/>).

- Take action (see: <www.opendoorsuk.org/about/how-we-help/advocacy>).

There is not enough space to write about all the wonderful work being done by churches and Christian organizations across the UK – we have simply highlighted a few examples here. There are so many other wonderful projects, such as Christians Against Poverty (CAP), Street Pastors, Street Angels, Restored, Kintsugi Hope, Hope for Justice, Eden Network (joineden.org), Foodbank, Linking Lives, Transforming Lives for Good (TLG), Home for Good, Care for the Family, Faith in Later Life and more. Check them out and see how you might pray for and support their work.

So the task to rebuild is before us. It's time for the Church to organize a party – a street party, where the Church acts as host and servant. Everyone is invited.

End note

This isn't so much a book as a *seed*. It's not an answer but a moment for reflection.

Restore
Renew
Rebuild

Our challenge is to embrace the opportunity we have now and make the changes needed for the future of the Church. Actively take into account all the things that need to be repented of and acted on. For each and every Jesus community, this will look different. What is necessary and appropriate for one might be entirely different for another.

The Church will not vanish. Christianity will not die. The public representation of it may change radically in the years to come, but Jesus is alive and well and will continue his ministry in the world with or without the Church. We are faced with the decision to either hold on to what we have now or work with Jesus towards his vision of the restoration of all things.

All things made new.

We do have a part to play, each and every one of us. This isn't a problem that the select few need to make some decisions about. It is for all Christians to get involved, to get their hands dirty, in the process of this kingdom restoration.

To do this effectively, we must ask ourselves some fundamental questions.

- 'Am I willing to be involved? Will I step up and play my part?'

- 'Will I offer what I have? Am I willing to use my own resources as part of this work?'
- 'Do I love Jesus enough to live fully for him and his work?'

The anointing

As noted in Part 3 of this book, Jesus started his ministry in Luke 4 by reading from the scroll of Isaiah 61. Also in Luke 4, Jesus stopped his reading of Isaiah 61 at verse 2, but everyone in the room knew the full prophecy in that passage, which speaks of ancient ruins being restored:

> The Spirit of the Sovereign LORD is on me,
>> because the LORD has anointed me
>> to proclaim good news to the poor.
> He has sent me to bind up the broken-hearted,
>> to proclaim freedom for the captives [slaves]
>> and release from darkness for the prisoners,
> to proclaim the year of the LORD's favour [forgiveness]
>> and the day of vengeance of our God [towards our enemies],
> to comfort all who mourn,
>> and provide for those who grieve in Zion –
> to bestow on them a crown of beauty
>> instead of ashes,
> the oil of joy
>> instead of mourning,
> and a garment of praise
>> instead of a spirit of despair.
> They will be called oaks of righteousness,
>> a planting of the LORD
>> for the display of his splendour.
>
> They will rebuild the ancient ruins
>> and restore the places long devastated;

they will renew the ruined cities
    that have been devastated for generations.
(Isaiah 61.1-4a)

This is the life of someone living in the Spirit, for Spirit-filled believers will demonstrate these things in their lives. All the wonderful attributes mentioned in Isaiah 61 are the overflow from and the fruits in the lives of people living with the resurrection spirit within them. At that point of saying 'Yes' to Jesus and receiving the Spirit, we are set apart as people who will . . .

- speak the gospel as real good news;
- patch up the battered and the bruised;
- recover sight for the blind;
- release the enslaved – self-enslaved or imposed;
- give new life to the ex-offenders and prisoners;
- announce God's freedom for all people;
- comfort those who have a broken heart;
- impart life over death;
- invite joy into the place of mourning;
- live as people who see God where others don't;
- see rubble but also see potential;
- bring life at its fullest to places devastated by previous generations;
- fully display their goodness from their God.

What a powerful vision for our lives!

Therefore, we commission, receive and anoint you, our readers, brothers and sisters, for this appointed time. We call you to your role in this restoration, renewing and rebuilding. Pray carefully to determine your part and walk boldly with us.

In Jesus, we see the fullness of this resurrection work that we now get to join. This vision of Jesus found in Isaiah, read out by Jesus in Luke 4 shows us three things.

- It presents the relevance of the gospel, both for the salvation of souls and in the bricks and mortar of lives.
- It challenges the status quo: things as they are now do not determine what they will become. God's Spirit will rock the boat, unsettling what we think is 'normal'.
- It offers hope that things will be better, that lives can improve, and the possibilities are endless.

As we end our time with you here, go forward. Willingly and intentionally say 'Yes' to this way of life, this Spirit-empowered ministry.

Write your name in the space provided on the following page and invite God to fill you with the Spirit for this divine purpose.

The Spirit of the Sovereign LORD is on me:

[add your name here] ....,

because the LORD has anointed me to . . .

- speak the gospel as real good news;
- patch up the battered and the bruised;
- recover sight for the blind;
- release the enslaved – self-enslaved or imposed slavery;
- give new life to the ex-offenders and prisoners;
- announce God's freedom for all people;
- comfort those who have a broken heart;
- impart life over death;
- invite joy into the place of mourning;
- live as someone who sees God where others don't;
- see rubble but also see potential;
- bring life at its fullest to places devastated by previous generations;
- fully display goodness from their God.

I will be a person who puts the life of Jesus on full display.

Amen.

Serve

Debra Green OBE

Publishing April 2022

Pre order at: spckpublishing.co.uk/serve-the-core-mission-of-the-body-of-christ

Paperback ISBN: 9780281086801   **eBook** ISBN: 9780281086818